POLITICS AND PHILOSOPHY

Philosophical Introductions

Series editors: Anthony Ellis and Gordon Graham

POLITICS AND PHILOSOPHY

*The Necessity and Limitations of Rational
Argument*

Stanley S. Kleinberg

BLACKWELL
Oxford UK & Cambridge USA

First published 1991

Basil Blackwell Ltd
108 Cowley Road, Oxford, OX4 1JF, UK

Basil Blackwell, Inc.
3 Cambridge Center
Cambridge, Massachusetts 02142, USA

British Library Cataloguing in Publication Data

A CIP catalogue record for this book is available from the British Library.

Library of Congress Cataloging in Publication Data
Kleinberg, Stanley S.
  Politics and philosophy: the necessity and limitations of rational
argument/Stanley S. Kleinberg.
    p. cm. – (Philosophical introductions)
  Includes bibliographical references and index.
  ISBN 0–631–16074–4: ISBN 0–631–16075–2 (pbk.)
  1. Political science – Philosophy.
I. Title. II. Series.
B65.K64 1991
320'.01–dc20   90–22730
                                                      CIP

Typeset in 11 on 13pt Garamond
by Photo·graphics Ltd, Honiton, Devon
Printed in Great Britain by T. J. Press Ltd, Padstow, Cornwall

Contents

For Sue, Daniel and Hugh

Preface

My thoughts on the relationship between politics and philosophy have been moulded by years of teaching both of these subjects. One of the attractions of both political theory and philosophy is that important and interesting questions arise at an early stage. Compared with science or history, beginners can fairly quickly put themselves in a position to have thoughts of their own on questions about which experts disagree. This has the happy consequence that academic practitioners of these subjects have a ready opportunity to learn from their students. In trying to show how thinking about political ideas can lead to an interest in philosophy, I have been much helped by the questions which my students have asked me.

I am grateful to colleagues and friends at Stirling with whom I have engaged in many hours of pleasurable discussion of the arguments discussed in this book. I am also indebted to the Series editors, particularly to Gordon Graham, for encouragement and criticisms. But of course I alone bear responsibility for obscurities, confusions and blunders.

Stanley S. Kleinberg
University of Stirling

December 1990

Part I
Introduction

1

Aims

The chief purpose of this book is to demonstrate how an interest in politics allied to an intellectually inquisitive temperament can lead people in the direction of philosophy. Probably most people who are interested in politics have, or have had, some partisan allegiances. To this general rule I am no exception. I was already a member of the Labour Party before I became a student and accustomed at election time to knocking on people's doors and asking them to vote for Labour candidates. Although in Britain the reaction of opponents is usually courteous, such canvassing is an activity to be recommended only to those who are confident in their opinions. My youthful certainty that I had a clear understanding of politics and that those who disagreed with me must be either insincere or gullible enabled me to tackle the work with a degree of enthusiasm. I always enjoyed the activity of arguing with opponents but I was also inclined to see such argument as no more than an opportunity for me to tell them where they had gone wrong.

However I long ago realized that those who disagreed with me were not all ignorant or contemptible any more than members of my own party were uniformly knowledgeable or admirable, and that I had lessons to learn, not just truths to impart, in argument with others. What I wish to draw attention to is less my own self-righteousness, which I should like to think has been long overcome, than the fact that the change in the certainty with which I hold most of my political opinions has been accompanied by only minor adjustments in the contents of these opinions. Although I no longer think of my political beliefs as ones which all those of goodwill will share, if only they take the trouble to think things through, the beliefs themselves have undergone no fundamental changes. So I remain a member of the Labour Party though now a rather inactive one. But if I do not think I can produce arguments for my political beliefs in a way that is bound to convince any fair-minded listener, what makes these opinions *mine*? Are they mine simply in the way for example that my support for a particular football team is mine? Yet my life-long enthusiasm for Tottenham Hotspur is simply a matter of taste rather than opinion. I do not think that it can or needs to be defended as correct. It has never occurred to me to suppose that those who prefer Arsenal are guilty of some intellectual error, or that I necessarily disagree with them about something, whereas if challenged I feel that I need to justify my political opinions. But how can I do this if I recognize that others can reject my opinions without going demonstrably wrong?

Apart from a certain curiosity which has led me to contemplate how I am related to my own political opinions, the thoughts which underlie this book have also been prompted by the way in which my students react to my attempts to teach political philosophy. Many have shown a keen interest in knowing my party allegiance. As is apparent, this is not something I attempt to keep secret. The reason why I always tell students who enquire is to alert them to the possibility of hidden bias. But why should I be so concerned to avoid bias? Why do I try to teach political philosophy in a way that places little emphasis on my own political opinions? If I was employed in a university to teach biology, my concern would surely be to signal those of my views which I knew to be controversial but ultimately to spend most of my time telling my students what I thought was correct and why I thought it was correct.

Are there good reasons for this cautious approach? One reason is that I know that most of my students already have firm political opinions and am anxious that they should not think of philosophical judgements as items to be selected simply because they happen to fit comfortably with existing political beliefs. But that anxiety would not exist if most of the students I encountered were politically uncommitted and seeking to make up their minds. Even in such changed circumstances however there might still be a reason why those who teach political philosophy ought to be cautious in the way they seek to argue for their own beliefs. This is because there may be something in the nature of political dispute that no matter how good the arguments we use to justify our conclusions, these will always remain contestable to an altogether different degree from that which applies to the conclusions of scientists. But is this true and if so why?

My hope is that this book will not merely demonstrate how philosophical questions can arise, but will also cast some light on how we can feel committed to our political opinions, whilst recognizing their essentially contestable nature. In order to do this I shall consider what kind of subject politics is. For that reason I shall draw frequent comparisons between political argument and argument in other spheres, such as science and religion, as well as between political activity and some other kinds of activity. This is especially the case in the first part of the book, where I argue that political beliefs are moral in character. I shall suggest also that normal political discourse presupposes the need for such beliefs to be supported by rational argument.

Thereafter Parts Two, Three and Four explore some of the arguments that are invoked within those traditions of political thought that are most frequently encountered, namely liberalism, conservatism and socialism. I shall consider two different varieties of liberalism and socialism as well as a very traditional conception of conservatism. The point of each of these discussions is not to offer a general survey of any of the political stances but to give some indication of the extent to which different political stances lend themselves to rational argument. I seek to bring out the nature of the good life, as viewed within each of the ideological traditions to be considered, and also how those who operate within each of these traditions conceive of the relationship between the community and its individual members.

In Part Five I seek to draw a general conclusion about the relationship between political argument and rationality. This will enable me to propose an answer to the question I raised above about whether political conclusions are always contestable and also to cast some light on the nature and importance of philosophy as an academic subject. It is a subject in which those who contemplate my conclusion will, whether they endorse it or reject it, hopefully have succeeded in taking a few steps.

2

Political and Philosophical Thinking

Politics as a Trouble-shooting Strategy

In the course of our lives we acquire beliefs about the world and how we ought to conduct ourselves. As young children we are for the most part ready to believe what we are told by those whom we love and trust. Thereafter and in varying degrees we may find ourselves beset by uncertainties. Although not knowing what to believe can be disturbing, help is often at hand in the form of strategies on which many of us feel able to rely for answers to the questions that trouble us or might otherwise have troubled us. Such strategies emanate from a rich variety of sources. These sources differ both in the manner in which answers are vouchsafed and in the range of questions they seek to address. Let us briefly take three quite disparate examples, namely fortune-telling, religion and science.

People usually consult fortune-tellers because they wish to have information that will enable them to make better decisions or come to terms with their worries. Normally the fortune-teller's speciality is to make statements about the health, wealth and romantic prospects of her clients and their associates. But does she have a reason for the messages she gives to her clients? Notice the ambiguity of this question. If fortune-tellers are cynical people whose predominant interest is in taking the public's money, they certainly have business reasons for making some predictions rather than others, since they will wish the clients to return for further consultations and to pass on enthusiastic recommendations to their friends. Such fortune-tellers would presumably aim to tell the clients what they wish to hear while taking care to avoid predictions so immediate and so precise that they may readily and rapidly be shown to be false.

But our enquiry whether the fortune-teller has reasons for what she does can be taken in a second and more interesting way. We might wish to know not about the fortune-teller's motivation for her predictions but whether there is a good reason for the predictions themselves. Here our interest is not in *explanation* but in *justification*. If our concern is to explain what the fortune-teller does then we are likely to be satisfied with an answer which is couched in terms of her motivation. But to seek to reach a conclusion about whether what she does is justified is to have an interest in determining whether we should give credence to the predictions. To this question some respond by asserting with vehemence that fortune-tellers can indeed provide a reliable source of information. But what is certain is that even if some fortune-tellers may have good reasons for the claims they make, these are not readily vouchsafed to sceptical enquirers. Those who seek not merely answers to particular questions, but to understand why they are offered particular answers, are well advised to keep their money and stay away from fortune-tellers.

Religious commitment is naturally quite unlike reliance on fortune-telling. Often the comfort that religion offers its adherents is to be found not in the answers offered to troubling questions but in ready acceptance of a universe filled with mysteries that mere human beings can never hope to unravel. Western religions offer a view of the universe according to which our own presence in it is seen as fulfilling some purpose. Some religions also offer us the prospect of being able, through prayer, devotion and leading what is held to be the appropriate kind of life, to influence our own future both in this world and also in some later existence.

Are there reasons, in the second of the two senses distinguished above, for relying on religion as a source of comfort in a disturbing world? Most ministers of religion recommend beliefs and values, not on the basis of some special personal gift or insight which they claim to have, but because these beliefs and values give expression to a particular view of the world. Their guidance also normally encompasses a much wider range of questions than fortune-tellers tackle. Not many people nowadays think it appropriate to treat Scripture as a source of authority on empirical questions such as planetary orbits or the origin of species. But because a religion normally involves a conception of the right way to live, many think of it as a source of the moral principles by which we should regulate our lives.

But what reason is there to see the world in the way recommended by believers or to accept the principles they endorse? Again we can recognize that many people have a motivational reason for belief, but our concern is with whether there is a justifying reason. Although many may be unable to make the initial act of faith on which religious belief is normally held to rest, at least religious reasoning is usually available for us all to assess for ourselves, in a way in which the basis of the predictions made by the fortune-teller is not.

Science is not concerned with telling us how to lead our lives, but with solving puzzles about why our world is the way it is, with telling us what presumptions we may make about how it will be in the future, and on occasion with specifying the changes we may be able to make to it. Science is ambitious in that it seeks to explain all observable phenomena. The scientist's interest is in unlocking, rather than taking refuge in, the mysteries of the universe. He is at pains to base his answers on evidence that is available to all and seeks to avoid anything comparable to the leap of faith that may be involved in religion. We may be tempted to suppose that scientists are concerned exclusively with questions that are amenable to proof. It would however be a mistake to treat science as a source of unfailingly correct answers. In fact we shall see later that science is at its most reliable when it debunks positive answers, often provided by other scientists, to puzzling questions and at its most fallible when it attempts to provide such answers. So even an Isaac Newton is eventually superseded by an Albert Einstein. Indeed scientists constantly seek to demonstrate that even their most distinguished predecessors, however hard they sought to be guided by the evidence, often went wrong because they misinterpreted it, or did not realize that it was incomplete.

Like science and religion, politics generates strategies for tackling troubling questions. In a somewhat different way from religion, it is bound up with moral principles which purport to help us decide our future conduct. Its distinctive subject matter is the proper arrangement of the communities in which we live. By a *community* I mean any large group of people who interact in a mutually dependent way with one another and who are to a significant degree regulated by collective decision-making. Such a community might be a nation, or all of the inhabitants of a particular territory, or a section of these inhabitants, for example all except those designated as slaves. This definition is not intended to capture how the term is generally used but merely to stipulate how I propose to use it. So what I call a community may often be described as a 'society' although that term also has other uses. What matters with any stipulative definition is simply that the intended meaning should be clear to all. Since I think that political communities are normally characterized by the existence of some *common* standards and assumptions, I prefer to talk about communities rather than societies. Communities sometimes are and sometimes are not attended by the elaborate structure of a modern state. Unless we have the space, temperament, resources and survival skills to live as hermits, we can only do as we wish with our own lives if we are part of a community in which others are to some extent ready to respect our desire to do so. So the importance of politics, at any rate for those who cannot live as hermits, is inescapable. In politics, as in religion and science, the exponents of particular beliefs place great emphasis on the arguments which purport to justify their conclusions, although, as in the case of religion, the arguments are frequently regarded as unconvincing by many to whom they are addressed.

What is the connection between the diverse strategies for dealing with disturbing questions and the activity of philosophizing? Is the resort to philosophy itself such a strategy? The point about the trouble-shooting strategies is that they are supposed to help people to avoid or surmount doubt. Sometimes prospective students imagine this to be true of philosophy. They wish to study the subject because they believe that it will help them to learn 'the meaning of life' or to 'know themselves'. Those with such hopes risk early disappointment because they soon learn that, far from providing ready answers, academic philosophy seems to emphasize difficulties. These include not just those which may be involved in answering the questions satisfactorily but often those involved in even understanding or articulating them.

We may best think of philosophy then not as itself a source of strategies for answering troubling questions, but as a discipline which is concerned with the critical scrutiny of such strategies. It is the function of philosophy to help us make sense of the world by enabling us to make up our minds as to when there is good reason, in the sense previously noted, for adopting one of the strategies. We can put this point in more scholarly language and say that philosophy as a subject is concerned with the rational appraisal of all claims to knowledge and to justified belief.

Sometimes philosophy is represented as a *second-order* discipline. *First-order* questions are held to be the ones we address when we seek to come to terms with our universe and how we should conduct our lives. The statements that we make when we engage in religious, scientific or political discourse are held to be first-order. *Second-order* questions are held to be ones that concern the status of our first-order discourse. The statements we make *about* rather than *within* religion, science or politics are thus taken to be second-order. So 'Jenny is good-natured because she was born under the sign of Aries' counts as a first-order pronouncement whereas 'astrological statements are not scientific' counts as second-order.

If we view philosophy entirely as a second-order discipline, we see it just as a spin-off from other subjects. If we approach it in this way we may avoid the danger referred to in chapter 1 of thinking of philosophical opinions as if they were items which we should select or reject simply on the basis of how well they match our first-order beliefs. So thinking of philosophy in this way may help us achieve detachment. On the other hand it may also lead us astray. If we think of philosophy as a second-order discipline, we may not expect our philosophical conclusions to affect our answers to first-order questions. But this would be a mistake. Some people take astrology seriously *because* they think it is a science. If for example philosophical argument persuades them not to view it as a science, they may have reason to abandon judgements such as 'Jenny is good-natured because she was born under the sign of Aries'. So philosophy certainly can make a difference to our choice of trouble-shooting strategy.

It is however correct to suppose that philosophers are concerned with thinking critically about just those matters that others are ready to take for granted. So for every area which has its own distinctive principles or methods of argument, there is at least potentially a corresponding branch of philosophy. Philosophy of religion and of science are thus important branches of the subject. But why then is there no philosophy of fortune-telling? Part of the answer is that the fortune-tellers are not willing for their craft to be subjected to public scrutiny. If they offered reasons for the particular predictions they make, which they and others were able to take seriously, then futurology might become of interest to philosophers.

Subjecting other people's assumptions to critical scrutiny is never a recipe for easy popularity. Seeking to engage in rational appraisal of assumptions to which others are strongly committed runs the risk of being seen as a deeply subversive activity. It was on account of such behaviour that Socrates was held to have corrupted the youth of Athens and was sentenced to death. But philosophy is not solely concerned with debunking. Although it is possible to read the Socratic dialogues and gain the impression that Socrates' objective was to use his dialectical skills to pour scorn on the beliefs of others, his predominant concern was to apply his critical method in order to get his fellow-citizens to look critically at their beliefs about virtues such as justice with a view to setting these beliefs on a secure basis.

Because political dispute, as we shall see, involves a distinctive kind of argument, we would expect to find that political philosophy is a well-developed discipline. But having rejected the view that philosophy is a second-order discipline, we may draw a distinction between two related enterprises. The first is the use of philosophical reflection with the aim of advancing more cogent, that is more rationally compelling, political arguments. The second consists in allowing our interest in political debate to guide us to learn something about the nature of rational argument itself. These enterprises are not mutually exclusive and we may well be interested in both. However what is usually meant by political philosophy is the first kind of activity. Anyone who has read any of the classic texts of political philosophy, such as Hobbes's *Leviathan*[1] or Locke's *Two Treatises of Government*[2] or contemporary works such as Rawls's *A Theory of Justice*[3] or Nozick's *Anarchy, State and Utopia*[4] is bound to notice that the argument proceeds from generalizations about the human condition to conclusions about the proper objectives of government.

Although what is argued in Parts Two, Three and Four may often suggest some conclusions which belong to the first sort of enterprise, our main concern in this book however is with the role of rational argument in politics. To that extent we shall be engaging in the latter kind of activity more than the former. We shall be looking at claims that are advanced in the course of familiar political argument and not just at those to be found in scholarly works of political theory. These claims are of course frequently contested. By focusing on how political beliefs may be criticized by opponents, I shall show how the constraints of rationality enter into politics. In doing this I hope to cast some light on the nature of philosophy.

Philosophy and the Importance of Definitions

Whenever we engage in philosophical discussion of politics or of any other subject, we have to pay close attention to definitions. Indeed we drew attention earlier in this chapter to two different senses of 'reason'. In the past philosophers have sometimes been accused of being obsessed with questions about the meaning of words to the exclusion of any interest in the ideas these words express. Certainly a concern with definition is sterile if allied to a 'logic-chopping' frame of mind which delights in exposing the alleged inadequacies in the way in which others formulate their opinions in preference to engaging in hard thought about the merits of these opinions. One can but despair at the poverty of imagination of anyone who holds that so-called philosophical questions are all either pseudo-questions or really just questions about the meanings of words. In the heyday of linguistic philosophy in the years preceding and following the Second World War, there were philosophers who certainly came perilously close to adopting just such an outlook. Whether or not they really did adopt it, what can be said with confidence is that such an outlook is totally at variance with the history of the subject and is nowhere to be found amongst contemporary philosophers.

Nevertheless words are important and *conceptual* analysis should be seen as an important part of philosophy, provided it is realized that it is only a part. However it is important to distinguish *concepts* from *terms*. *Terms* are simply linguistic expressions. *Concepts* are not parts of a language but are the ideas that underlie any language. For example, the word 'party' in English can be used to refer to the kind of social event to which most of us like to be invited from time to time but also to a familiar kind of political organization. Here one and the same *term* is used on different occasions to express different *concepts*. We may also observe that the French word for 'party' in the political sense is 'parti' and the German word is 'Partei'. 'Party', 'parti' and 'Partei' are thus words that may be used in different languages to convey the same idea. Here different *terms* are used to express one and the same *concept*. Provided it is understood that the philosopher's concern is with concepts rather than terminology, it can be seen that the underlying concern is to make use of a tool for pursuing, not avoiding, an interest in ideas.

It is also on occasion useful to talk about *conceptions*. Concepts like all ideas are subject to the interpretation of those who make use of them. So although politicians as different as President Ronald Reagan and President Daniel Ortega of Nicaragua were both inclined to talk about democracy, we might suppose that the word did not have exactly the same meaning for each of them. Of course some would say that that is because one or other of them was grossly ignorant of the true nature of democracy. Others might suspect that one or other of them was only pretending to believe in democracy. Another possibility however is that the concept of democracy is itself sufficiently fuzzy to allow the different interpretations of Reagan and Ortega. Perhaps they were simply employing different conceptions of democracy. To say this would not commit us to saying that both should be regarded as

democrats, for such a judgement would reflect our own conception of democracy. We would be saying only that both Reagan
and Ortega had the concept of democracy, but that they interpreted the political requirements of democracy in different ways.
The difference between them should therefore not be seen as a
semantic one.

By contrast some apparently political disagreements may just
be examples of people using the same term to express ideas that
do not in fact conflict. So one person might claim that a particular
American naval officer was responsible for the shooting-down in
July 1988 of an Iranian passenger airliner, meaning that the officer
was at fault, and another person might say that the United States
government was responsible, meaning that it was appropriate for
the government to pay compensation. In this case we can see that
the two claims, although different, are quite compatible with one
another and indeed that the first claim might even be made in
support of the second. The appearance of conflict is thus super-
ficial because there are two different concepts of responsibility in
play.

In the case of democracy the reason why there is a case for
operating with a concept which is sufficiently fuzzy to allow
sharply competing interpretations is connected with the way in
which elements of both *fact* and *value* enter into the judgements
we make. There is, we often suppose, a radical distinction between
reality and what is desirable. Our factual judgements reflect the
world as we take it to be whereas our evaluative judgements relate
to the world as we think it ought to be. Moreover, we may be
tempted to assume, evaluative judgements must always be logically
independent of factual judgements. This is sometimes thought
to be the purport of David Hume's famous dictum about the
impossibility of ever deriving an 'ought' proposition from an 'is'
proposition.[5]

Although the distinction between fact and value is a useful one
to draw, we should not make the error of taking values to be
totally independent of facts. Imagine an argument about whether
John is a bully. Is this question factual or evaluative? There is
clearly both a factual and an evaluative element. It makes no sense
to call John a bully unless we believe that he has attempted to

impose his will on someone weaker than himself. But the truth of such a description of John's behaviour is not sufficient to make him a bully. Sometimes we may think that John has justification for imposing his will on someone weaker than himself. For example when polite requests have proved ineffective, John may secure the peace and quiet he needs to do his homework by hitting his noisy younger brother. In these circumstances not everyone will agree that his actions are those of a bully. There is always some scope for disagreement about what precise forms of behaviour constitute bullying.

The concept of democracy resembles that of a bully in that it has both an evaluative and a descriptive element. If we say that a particular state is governed democratically, we will normally be understood to be making a favourable evaluation of the way its affairs are conducted. But we also commit ourselves to the truth of some factual statement about popular input into that state's decision-making. Different conceptions of democracy reflect different value judgements about the precise way in which government must reflect the will of the people. If we recognize that these competing judgements can be made in good faith, then we may be ready to accept a fuzzy concept of democracy. By contrast other political concepts, such as that of an election or a parliament, are much less fuzzy. So although we would not be too surprised to find politically well-informed people (Marxists perhaps) who disagree about whether the United Kingdom, Australia and New Zealand are all democratically governed countries, we would not expect them to disagree about whether 1987 was a year in which parliamentary elections took place in each of the United Kingdom, Australia and New Zealand. This, we are inclined to say, is a demonstrable historical fact.

Just as concepts are sometimes too fuzzy, it is also possible for them to suffer from the opposite defect of being too precise for the job in hand. For example British judges have often told juries that they should not convict an accused person unless they are certain of his guilt beyond 'reasonable doubt'. No detailed guidance is normally given as to what kind of doubt is 'reasonable'. A justification for this is that the rationale for the jury system requires juries themselves to decide what is reasonable. Our conclusion should surely be with Aristotle that 'it is the mark of an educated man to look for precision in each class of things just so far as the nature of the subject admits'.[6]

So conceptual fuzziness does not always need to be avoided, but what is necessary is that we should be alert to such fuzziness. Undetected fuzziness leads to political arguments being conducted at cross purposes, as when people express what appear to be opposed views about freedom of religion because they have different understandings of whether Satanism is a religion. A comparable conceptual hazard is the use of what may be described as incomplete concepts, such as freedom or equality. These are concepts which cannot be properly understood without a specification of underlying variables. Consider the simple assertion (or denial) of the claim that all persons ought to be treated equally, where this is unaccompanied by any indication of what is held to constitute equal treament. In relation to tax liability, does it mean that all should pay the same amount of income tax, that everyone should pay the same proportion of their income in tax, that all should be be taxed so as to leave them with the same after-tax income, or simply that taxation law, whatever it happens to be, should be applied impartially to all? Each of these four possibilities, and perhaps others too, may strike us as ones for which a case might be made. What is futile is for someone to dismiss the different options as matters of detail but assert that the important thing is to be in favour of (or against) the principle of equal treatment. To such a person we may object that his underlying concept of equality is so incomplete that his position is not intelligible. Any opinion he expresses about equality will be empty of content.

What we have seen are some of the different ways in which the unwary may be confused by conceptual pitfalls. The philosopher's concern in defining concepts is not the pursuit of linguistic orthodoxy, but ensuring that the concept is suited to the task which it is required to perform. In making such a judgement, philosophers must necessarily attend to the world beyond philosophy. Take for example the concept of *phlogiston*. Eighteenth-century scientists knew that after an object, such as a stick or a lump of coal, had been heated for some time, it had a smaller mass than previously. From this they deduced the existence of a substance with negative weight called phlogiston which was involved in the process of combustion. Now however we know that the concept of phlogiston is to be discarded as a useful concept, except from the perspective of the historian of science, because it does not yield an accurate understanding of the phenomenon of combustion. There is thus a reciprocal relationship between the philosopher's concern with definition and the concern of those who are interested in the field which the philosopher seeks to examine. So it would be foolish to imagine that we could do worthwhile work in the philosophy of a given subject, without having some practical understanding of what goes on in that subject. When we contemplate science or history or politics, we may be led astray because we operate with inadequate concepts. Equally we might do bad philosophy because we lack a good enough grasp of the task that the concepts are asked to perform in the world beyond philosophy. It is essential that political philosophers know something of politics.

3

Definitions of Politics

Our discussion of the importance of concepts and definitions suggests that we need a definition of politics. Some might be inclined to discount this concern as unnecessarily pedantic. Do we not all really know already what politics is? Should we not therefore devote our energies to argument about what political conclusions should be drawn, rather than waste time on the explication of the concept of politics?

Such an attitude reminds me of a story told about William Whiteley, the Chief Whip in Britain's first post-war Labour Government. At that time the Labour Party sought to establish a code of discipline for its Members of Parliament which required them always to vote for the Party's official position, except on matters of conscience. But what exactly was a matter of conscience? Predictably some members of the Party establishment took a narrower view of this conceptual question than many of their followers on the backbenches. The Chief Whip was supposed to have said that a matter of conscience was like an elephant in that although he could not define it, he felt sure that he would recognize one when he saw it. Many of us, I suspect, think of politics in just this way; we may not know how to define it, but we feel sure that we can recognize it when we encounter it.

There is however an important respect in which the concept of politics (and for that matter that of conscience) is unlike that of an elephant. Given a clear enough view, a jury of linguistically competent, normally sighted, honest, sane and sober observers will agree about whether a given object is an elephant. In theory, one might concede, there could be difficult cases. So the jury

might well be divided if we confronted them with a woolly mammoth, but, since we are unable to do this, their task is in practice easy. However they might well disagree, in practice and not merely in theory, about what is political. Is the ritual of the daily salute to the flag by American schoolchildren political? When youths throw stones or other missiles at the police in disturbances in Baku or Belfast or Jerusalem or Johannesburg, are they acting politically? If the Pope calls for disarmament, is he making a political pronouncement? When English cricketers toured South Africa just before the release of Nelson Mandela in 1990, were their actions political? All of these questions are ones about which the members of our jury may disagree.

When we find that people are inclined to apply concepts in different ways, it becomes appropriate to seek definitions. In all cases we need to bear in mind what we take to be the point behind our understanding of a given concept. The above examples suggest a number of concerns that may be relevant to the concept of politics. The first is motive. For some people whether an action is political might depend on the reasons for which it is performed. So we might say that someone who went to play cricket in South Africa in order to express his support for apartheid certainly acted politically. But of course not all political actions are consciously political, any more for example than all criminal actions are consciously criminal. In any case the observation that political actions are those which are the product of political motives presupposes that we already know how such motives differ from non-political ones.

More illuminating is a second suggestion that our decision to see an action or practice as political connects up with our answer to the question 'Whose business is it?'. So to see a question as political may be to view it not just as the proper concern of a small number of private citizens, but as the business of all citizens or alternatively perhaps of those who are thought to be specially qualified to act on behalf of all citizens, for example the elected representatives of a community. So if we say that cricketers who toured South Africa were behaving politically, we might mean that their decision should not be seen as one that concerned only themselves and those who wished to play against them or watch them play, but a much wider public. On the other hand if we say that a religious leader is behaving politically, we may mean that he is concerning himself with questions that are more appropriately left to those who are the representatives of the community as a whole, or perhaps that he is acting as the mouthpiece of a government or a political party.

The third concern is one of perspective. To see something as political may be to presuppose a particular context or framework in terms of which it should be viewed. If someone suggests that the salute to the flag is political, he might mean that this is no harmless classroom ritual but an example of children being manipulated or indoctrinated by a government. The appropriate framework invoked here is that of promoting what is held to be an aggressively nationalistic culture. Similarly someone who claims that violence against the police is political may perhaps be inviting us to agree either that it is justified in the context of a repressive state or alternatively that it should be seen as something more sinister than mere hooliganism because it constitutes an assault on the foundations of life in the community. Thus different understandings of the concept of politics may reflect different priorities and perspectives and this we may illustrate by considering three different definitions of politics.

Politics: The Participant's Conception

The first person to write about politics in a systematic way was Aristotle. Previously some questions of enduring interest, about issues such as the nature of justice and of the state, had been discussed by Plato especially in *The Republic*.[1] Aristotle was one of Plato's pupils, and his book, *The Politics*,[2] published in the fourth century BC, can be seen as the very first work of political science. According to the first chapter of *The Politics* the political association is that which is the most 'sovereign and inclusive'[3] in its territory. The nearest contemporary equivalent to this association is the state, although of course the Ancient Greeks inhabited city-states rather than nation-states. So in effect Aristotle defines politics as that which concerns the running of the state.

The significance of this definition thus depends on the underlying conception of the role of the state. It will be quite uninformative to us if we are inclined to think of the state simply as the political organization of the community for we cannot without circularity define politics in terms of the state and the state in terms of politics. Aristotle's position however is not circular because his reference to the sovereignty and inclusiveness of the *polis* is an indication of a particular conception of the role of the state. The choice of these epithets indicates not simply that he viewed the state as the supreme legislative body, but also as the appropriate body to regulate any matter which arises in any part of the community. The all-embracing nature of this definition invites comparison with East European constitutional provisions that once sought to guarantee the 'leading role' of the Communist Party. The point about these provisions was not merely that the activities of other parties were banned, but that they expressed the claim that the Communist Party could appropriately regulate all aspects of life within the community. If we try to envisage the Aristotelian *polis* in the modern world, it would be competent to determine whether women might be ordained as ministers of religion, what time children should go to bed and how much fibre we all ought to eat each day. In practice the *polis* might not attempt to settle every question but Aristotle would have had no sympathy with the claim made for example by contemporary defenders of the right to privacy that some matters are no business of the state. His is thus a totalitarian view, which would be rejected by many, although its illiberal nature is tempered by his view that in practice the best governed *polis* is one in which all citizens take a turn in governing. This however still excludes those whom Aristotle thought fit only to be slaves.

Observe that this account of politics reflects a view about human nature. In Book I of *The Politics* Aristotle asserts that man is a political animal.[4] This is not intended to mean that people are on the whole likely to seek power over others or that they tend to be interested in current affairs. Aristotle's claim is far more ambitious. He thought that human identity was bound up with being a citizen, or as Aristotle termed it, a part of the *polis*, and indeed that personal excellences could only be attained within the *polis*. He claimed that 'the man who is isolated – who is unable to share in the benefits of political association, or has no need to share because he is already self-sufficient – is no part of the polis and must therefore be either a beast or a god'.[5] Thus to be detached from the political process is on this view not to be properly human. So Aristotle's account of the relationship between the community and the individual citizen is an indication not merely of particular political opinions, but also of a particular understanding of the place of politics in human existence.

Convictions about the proper direction of policy also shape the definitions of politics offered by contemporary political theorists. Take for example that proposed by Bernard Crick. In his opinion 'politics . . . can be simply defined as the activity by which differing interests within a given unit of rule are conciliated by giving them a share in power in proportion to their importance to the welfare and the survival of the whole community'.[6] We observed in chapter 2 that a philosopher's concern with definition is quite different from that of a lexicographer. The concern of the latter is to tell us how a term is generally employed, whereas the striking feature of Crick's definition is that it is intended as a suggestion about how the term should be used. If we accept Crick's proposal, then we will no longer characterize as political much activity which is commonly so described. The history of the twentieth century, from Hitler and Stalin to Pol Pot and Ceausescu, has yielded numerous examples of people who have been thought of as political leaders but who have had no time whatsoever for conciliation and have sought instead to eradicate those interests which they have seen as inimical to their own plans. Indeed even those whose objectives and methods are less extreme may prefer not conciliation but a clear victory over important interests within the community. For example it might be argued that when Mrs Thatcher came to power in the United Kingdom in 1979 her objective was not to conciliate the Trade Unions in accordance with their importance to the survival and welfare of the whole community, but to confront them in order to diminish that importance.

It is clear then that Crick's definition of politics presupposes a view of how the affairs of a community *ought* to be conducted.

In particular he favours conciliation rather than confrontation. Although such political opinions are a long way from the totalitarian ones of Aristotle, what is common to each is that their definitions of politics reflect underlying values. We may say that each subscribes to a *participant's conception* of politics, in that each embodies a contestable view about the scope or point of political activity.

Politics: The Observer's Conception

Is there an alternative to adopting a participant's conception of politics? Consider the following proposal by the American political scientist Robert A. Dahl. He writes that 'a political system is any persistent pattern of human relationships that involves, to a significant extent, power, rule, or authority'.[7] This is a different kind of definition from the ones previously considered. Whereas Aristotle and Crick both proposed definitions that reflect contestable ideas which embody political values, Dahl's definition aspires to be value-neutral in that it might be accepted by fascists, liberals, communists, anarchists or anyone. We may say that Dahl operates with an *observer's conception* of politics.

Even within Dahl's definition, however, it is possible to see a practical dimension which reflects a generous view of the ambit of political science. We can imagine that other social scientists, sociologists for example, might accuse Dahl of a kind of intellectual imperialism in that it looks as if whatever takes the fancy of the political scientist looking around for something to research can, on Dahl's definition, be claimed to be political. So decision-making within a university, a multinational corporation, a church or a family can all be argued as falling within the province of politics, and hence of the political scientist. It can be maintained that the wide scope of Dahl's definition is to be regarded as a weakness. The problem is that although it includes everything that anyone is ever tempted to classify as political, it also includes an enormous segment of behaviour which no-one has previously been disposed to regard as political.

Assessing Competing Definitions

We have now looked at three different definitions of politics, observed how these definitions can be seen as complementary to particular assumptions, and seen how each proposed definition might be viewed by some as unsatisfactory. Where does this lead us? I suggested earlier that our concepts need to be well matched to the functions they are required to perform. So definitions of politics are to be assessed not as right or wrong but as more or less appropriate to the task in hand. What complicates matters is that we cannot assume agreement about what that task is. Indeed the task may be different on different occasions. As a leading biologist has pointed out, whether we classify lobster as fish depends on whether we approach the question as biologists, fishermen or gourmets.[8] No answer to the conceptual question can be regarded as correct independently of the nature of our interest in it. What applies to the concept of fish applies equally to that of politics.

When we approach the matter in this way, it is easy to see that an observer's definition is indeed appropriate for the political scientist. The reason is that the function of that discipline is not to convince us of the desirability of any given view of how the affairs of a community ought to be regulated, but to enable us to understand what such views involve and in what circumstances they gather support and tend to be implemented. Since the point of their work is to explain, political scientists need to discount as irrelevant their own opinions about how a community should be governed. Indeed although it might be a hopeless enterprise for anyone to seek an understanding of the politics of a society with which he was totally out of sympathy, political scientists do not even need to be members of the community they are studying.

Understood in this way, political science is a secondary activity. The primary activity is undertaken by those who express opinions about how the community ought to be governed and seek to implement these opinions. About such matters people often *disagree*. This concept is an important one. If two people disagree with one another, they hold not just different but incompatible opinions or attitudes. They cannot both be right, although they might both be wrong. There are many differences which do not constitute disagreements. If I like the taste of garlic and you hate it, we may have different attitudes to garlic but there is nothing which need lead either of us to believe that the other has made any kind of mistake. However on matters on which we believe we disagree, each believes the other to be wrong and in most cases each supposes himself to have a reason for maintaining that the other is wrong.[9]

Before discussing the nature and significance of political disagreement, we should note that because politics is an area of discourse within which disagreement is common, we cannot hope to propose any participant's definition of politics and expect it to command general assent. From an observer's perspective however we may say that *politics is that area of human activity which is undertaken in pursuance of any participant's definition of how the affairs of a community ought to be regulated*. Such a definition will serve the purposes of political science. It means for example that the Ayatollah Khomeini and Ronald Reagan were both involved in politics, even though they would not have agreed about whether one person's decision to order their life without regard to the precepts of the Koran was the legitimate business of other members of the community. It also serves my own purpose since my objective resembles that of the political scientist in that I am primarily concerned to say something *about* political activity and argument rather than to make a contribution *to* such activity or argument. For present purposes competing participant's definitions can be viewed as rival conceptions of politics. This is not to say that my definition of politics is more correct or more fundamental than any of the participant's conceptions. To say that would be like adopting the fisherman's perspective on whether to count lobster as fish, and then concluding that biologists are mistaken because they claim that lobster are not fish. In fact my definition, because it is an observer's definition, would not get off the ground if others did not have clear views about what constitutes the affairs of a community and how these ought to be regulated.

4

Arguments, Reasons and Morality

The following is a not untypical exchange between Party leaders in the House of Commons.

> *Mr Kinnock*: . . . absolutely nobody can reasonably be expected to accept what the Prime Minister has said.
>
> Is it not a fact that she is trying to hide what the outcome of the proposals will be, and that she is ashamed of her proposals? Can she not give figures? Is she afraid? Is she innumerate or simply mendacious?
>
> *Mrs Thatcher*: No, Mr Speaker, factual. There has been an annual uprating of social security benefits for many years. That is the fact. It is only the rt. hon. gentleman who is capable of ignoring the facts. He cannot be expected to be believed if he does.[1]

Everyone knows that politicians as in the example just quoted spend a lot of time arguing. Most of us understand 'argument' as equivalent to 'row' or 'altercation'. Undoubtedly politicians, at any rate in a multi-party system, spend a lot of time in what are often seen as tedious assertions that their opponents are stupid or dishonourable. Many members of the public are appalled by the insulting nature of so many political exchanges, but they should not be surprised. Partly this is because it is natural for those who seek to win or retain power to wish to emphasize what differentiates them from their competitors. Partly it is because the disparagement of those whom one believes to be wrong is a widespread human attribute. Politicians do this in a particularly public way, but others like academics and theologians are also capable of taking a most unflattering view of colleagues with whom they disagree. Whenever we are confident that we are right and others are wrong, there is a temptation to suppose that they must be either fools or knaves.

There is however another and more important sense in which politics involves argument, and that is the impersonal sense in which we may think of an argument as something independent of the actual process of arguing. This is the sense in which we recognize the existence of arguments for or against pursuing particular policies, quite independently of our identifying particular instances of anyone actually putting forward the argument. Conceived in this way an argument for doing something is simply a chain of reasoning whose conclusion amounts to what may be seen as a *reason* for action. Such reasons can be compared with reasons for believing factual propositions. Historians and scientists constantly propound arguments for accepting claims about what happens or has happened and how it is to be explained. Political arguments yield conclusions about what should be done and good political arguments thus constitute reasons for action. These may be thought to be different from reasons for believing factual propositions in that even when we think we have a good reason for supporting a particular course of action, we might still hesitate about claiming that our view about what ought to be done is *true*. For the moment we shall simply take note of this potential complication.

The concept of a reason is employed in the paragraph above in the second of the two senses of reason distinguished in chapter 2. A reason in this sense is something of which people may in fact take no account, but which it would have been *reasonable* for them to take into account. So in earlier centuries few if any doubted that the earth was flat. But we might argue that there was reason for them to have entertained some doubts, because they were able to observe that the mast was the last part of a ship to disappear over the horizon and were unable to explain this phenomenon. Similarly Britain and France had reason to build up their military strength in the 1930s after Hitler had signalled his aggressive intentions in the pages of *Mein Kampf*, but many British and French politicians failed to recognize this. It should be noted however that even this more impersonal sense of reason is backed up by an implicit understanding as to what is reasonable, and our judgements here must reflect our understanding of the circumstances of those whom we are judging. So we could scarcely argue that people living in the Bronze Age had reason to believe that the world was round, any more than we could claim that Hitler's victims had reason to kill him whilst he was still a child. We always have to make a judgement about what people can be expected to make of the evidence available to them. But since human beings are at best imperfectly rational, they do not always believe what they have good reason to believe or do what they have good reason to do. It should be emphasized however that some reasons are more conclusive, or more nearly conclusive, than others. Hence a mere failure to do or believe what one has some reason to do or believe does not of itself prove that one has behaved either less rationally than one should have done or, as we say in the more extreme cases, irrationally. Reasons can conflict with one another and are thus often presumptive rather than conclusive. Juries in criminal trials are frequently presented by the prosecution lawyer with reasons for believing in the guilt of the accused and by the defence lawyer with reasons for believing in his innocence. A jury does not necessarily display defective rationality if it acquits a man of murder even though his finger-prints are the only ones on the murder weapon, since there can be an innocent explanation for this fact. But it is a failure of rationality if the jurors do not recognize the fingerprint evidence as a relevant factor which, other things being equal, should point them in the direction of conviction rather than acquittal. In general rational people match their actions and beliefs to the weight of the available reasons.

We have now developed a chain of conceptual connections. Politics involves arguments, arguments involve reasons, and these reasons are reasons why particular courses of action ought to be pursued. These connections suggest two questions. The first is whether there really can be conclusive political arguments to which we can appeal in order to show that there is a rational justification for particular policies. I plan however to postpone consideration of this question until later. The second question arises from the use of the term *ought*, which typically we use in making moral judgements. Are political judgements a species of moral judgement?

Politics and Morality

The chain of conceptual connections can be presented in the form of an argument.

(A)   Politics involves arguments.

(B)   An argument (in the relevant sense) concludes with the claim that there is a good reason for acting in a particular way.

(C)   We ought to act in accordance with good reasons.

(D)   Therefore politics involves the claim that we ought to act in particular ways.

This argument does not as it stand conclusively demonstrate that there is a connection between politics and morality. In support of (B) and (C) I have offered an account of a conceptual connection (1) between arguments and reasons and (2) between rationality and a willingness to act on the basis of good reasons. This does of course presuppose a commitment to rationality, but that as we shall see is implicit in the nature of argument. For the moment (A) has merely been asserted. I intend to complement this assertion with an account of why politicians *need* to engage in arguments. But in any case even if the premises are accepted as true and even if the conclusion can be validly derived from them, it still does not follow that political arguments are moral in character. Even if it is accepted that politics issues in 'ought' judgements, it might still be thought to be independent of morality, because it is clear that only some 'ought' judgements are moral in character. Consider these claims in the way in which we would normally interpret them:

(1)   We ought never to torture prisoners.

(2)   The President ought to have known that Jean-Jacques Rousseau was not born in France.

(3) Jill ought to go to the dentist.

It will be apparent that the first claim will normally be held to express a moral judgement, but that the other two do not. The President's ignorance and Jill's failure to have gone to the dentist might be judged as something other than moral faults. If someone makes the second claim, we expect him to be able to back it up by citing some authoritative and readily accessible work of reference which will indicate where Rousseau was born. So (2) expresses a claim about what attention to the evidence should have led the President to believe. The President's alleged failure is thus one of rationality and is similar to that of the medieval flat-earthers, in that a mistaken belief is entertained despite the availability of evidence that it is a mistake. There are of course occasions when we think that a failure to know something is a moral failure. For example a failure to be aware that a recently bereaved person is liable to be hurt by a joke about funerals is indicative of a defect in the moral character of the person who makes it. Similarly if the President had set himself up as an expert on Rousseau and then misled others because he had not taken enough trouble to acquaint himself with the available literature, we might think that there was some moral failure involved. But plainly ignorance of Rousseau's background would not normally count as a moral failing, since a person's moral character generally bears no relation to his competence as a Rousseau scholar.

The final claim might be thought to be more concerned with prudence than rationality, but imprudence too is a kind of irrationality. The point here is that the speaker presumably imagines that Jill is suffering from toothache, and believes that she is or should be aware that toothache which is ignored is likely to lead to greater suffering. So Jill is accused of failure to do what rationally she ought to do. But although Jill may be foolish in not going to the dentist, she does not act dishonourably and her failure, though maybe a failure of nerve, is not a moral one.

My present object however is not to engage in a full discussion of the conceptual analysis of 'ought' judgements, but simply to indicate that moral *oughts* can be distinguished from rational *oughts*. So the *oughts* in (2) and (3) do not entail moral judgements.

If we are to conclude that politics involves morality, we shall need to be convinced that politicians do more than appeal to rationality or prudence. If it is clear that politicians commonly make use of arguments which are moral rather than merely rational or prudential and we can reinforce this with an account of why they are constrained to do this, then a good case will have been made for the claim that political assertions are moral.

It is apparent from political oratory that many politicians take a somewhat elevated view of their work. 'Ask not what your country will do for you but what you can do for your country' demanded John F. Kennedy. Even Harold Wilson, widely perceived as a supreme pragmatist, once said that the British Labour Party was a moral crusade or it was nothing. Politicians generally claim that their conception of the good of the community is such as to demand the moral support of all citizens. Even those least disposed to engage in lofty rhetoric are apt, when they have won an election or otherwise attained power, to claim that it is the duty of all loyal honourable citizens to obey the government. Detailed argument about whether and when citizens owe such loyalty are in normal times left well alone by politicians and are largely the province of political philosophers. This is but one example of the philosopher's habit of examining assumptions that others tend to take for granted. I shall not pursue such arguments here. What I wish to draw attention to is not the problem of justifying claims of this kind, but the significance of the fact that such claims are made.

Given our definition of politics, the moral claims that governments make of their citizens should come as no surprise. Even though politicians may disagree about what constitutes the good of the community, and even in some cases about who constitutes the community, politics revolves around the concern of bringing about the good of a community. It is plain that no conception of the good of a community can be attained without power. Politicians aspire to be able to get large numbers of individuals to accept arrangements, such as respecting other people's property or paying taxes, which, considered *in isolation*, are damaging to their own interests. When I say of an idea that it is to be considered in isolation, I mean that it is to be considered in the narrowest possible social context. So for example paying money in tax would normally count, considered in isolation, as contrary to a citizen's interests, even if he approves of the benefits that are funded out of the taxation and supports the idea that taxation is the appropriate way for the benefits to be funded.

The practical problem of getting people to do things which considered in isolation are contrary to their interests and which they might thus prefer not to do, is not uniquely a problem for politicians and governments. It might on occasion be viewed as a problem for traders who earn their living providing goods and services to the public. The trader obviously needs the customer to pay for the goods or services required, and payment for goods or services, considered in isolation, is no more in the consumer's interest than paying taxes is in that of the citizen. For the trader however the problem is usually a minor one. He is normally dealing with a customer who has chosen out of self-interest to deal with him, and who will often wish to continue to do business with him. It is quite likely therefore that she will be happy to pay him, and is not even tempted to view the payment in isolation. Depending on what business the trader is in and the value of the transaction, he may also take security measures designed to ensure that the customer simply cannot benefit from the goods or services he provides without payment. Both parties also know that in the last resort the law would seek to enforce payment. Consequently the more important problem for the trader may be to persuade a potential customer to do business with him in the first place, rather than to persuade her to pay up. But governments are dealing with subjects, who at any rate as individuals, have not chosen to do business with them.

This suggests that a more appropriate though somewhat unflattering comparison is between the demands of government and those of criminals, such as blackmailers and extortionists. The activities of such criminals resemble those of government ministers at least to the extent that they share a logistical problem in that each is in the business of making demands of people who have not freely chosen to do business with them. The task of the blackmailer or extortionist is however simpler than that confronting the politician in that the former merely requires the compliance of a limited number of individuals for a limited length of time, sometimes of only one person and for no longer than it takes to transfer a bundle of banknotes. Consequently such criminals have a reasonable chance of attaining their ends by means of threats, inducements and deception. Such stratagems may be sufficient to induce the victim to consider the criminal's demand for money not in isolation, but in relation to the special circumstance which the criminal creates. So if a gunman says to me, 'Hand over your wallet or I shoot!' I may be persuaded that his proposal, which in isolation is highly unattractive, should be viewed in a context in which the alternative is the loss of both my life and my wallet, which seems even less attractive.

The kind of stratagem which the criminal uses may also be employed by governments and politicians. The government may induce the citizen to pay his tax bill by threatening punishment. But the politician's task is altogether more formidable than that of the criminal because he needs to influence large numbers of people over long periods of time. So when confronted with recalcitrant subjects who demand to know what good reason there is why they should do what seems, and when viewed in isolation usually is, contrary to their interest, the politician who seeks to govern a community needs to supplement his enforcement measures with an answer. He cannot content himself with an appeal to the subject's self-interest, for governments require obedience and conformity even from those who believe that their interest would best be served by the government's defeat.

So governments have to persuade their subjects that their demands are legitimate. Even the most autocratic political system cannot long endure unless at least some people accept its legitimacy, for no-one can intimidate all of the people all of the time. Idi Amin was popular with the lower ranks of the army from which he had emerged, Pol Pot commanded the loyalty of the Khmer Rouge and Ceausescu had the support of the Securitate. So the politician who wishes to exercise power must attempt to persuade citizens that they ought to support his attempts to realize the good of the whole community.

It is true that where sectarian or ethnic divisions are important, politicians may not always address themselves in this way to all citizens. Often the politician's conception of the community may entirely exclude some who would like to see themselves as citizens. For example until recently Afrikaner politicians in South Africa resisted demands that blacks be given political rights with the claim that they should really be considered as citizens of separate allegedly independent countries like Bophuthatswana. Everywhere however politicians in effect say to at least some citizens 'Support me because I am seeking to bring about the good of a community to which you owe allegiance.' Once in power they ask those who have not hitherto supported them to obey their laws, because these allegedly embody the will of the people. This is clearly different from an appeal to rational self-interest. It is also entirely vacuous unless it can be backed up with argument. If someone seeks simply to coerce me or to bribe me to do as he wants, I have a decision to make but I am not confronted with the claim that it would be public-spirited for me to do as I am told or dishonourable for me to stand my ground and refuse. But once someone asserts that what he demands of me amounts to a requirement which it would be dishonourable or selfish for me not to accede to, I can ask why he believes this and expect him to advance arguments.

To appeal to the honour of citizens or their public-spiritedness is of course to make a moral appeal. If we fail to act honourably or in a public-spirited way, then this is a failure of moral character, and quite different from ignorance of some well-attested historical fact or omitting to pay a timely visit to the dentist. So politicians are committed to the deployment of moral ideas and argument in a way that criminals are not. Needless to say it does not follow that politicians cannot *also* be crooks or gangsters. But even the least respectable of them differs from those who are *merely* crooks or gangsters. The Mafia is not a political organization because, although it may be very influential and able to make plausible threats to bury its more irksome opponents in concrete, the *Mafiosi* do not advance any ideas about what constitutes good government or what constitutes a citizen's duty. I do not seek to cast any aspersion on the sincerity of most politicians, but simply to draw attention to the fact that even the most cynical of them still need to be committed to deploying moral ideas and argument.

5

The Status of Political Judgements

Necessary and Contingent Propositions

Our conclusion that politicians are committed to the use of moral argument leaves open the important issue of whether the disputes about which they argue can in fact be rationally resolved. An enduring concern of philosophers has been to determine the appropriate way to settle different kinds of intellectual problem. The history of the subject has included attempts to draw up a classification system for different types of statement in accordance with the ways of establishing whether they should be accepted. A traditional move, made in different terms by Leibniz, Descartes and Hume, was to distinguish the *necessary* from the *contingent*. Propositions were said to be necessary if they were true in any imaginable universe and contingent if their truth depended on some property of the universe as we in fact experience it.[1] Necessary truths were thus viewed as ones which could be known independently of actual observations. Once such a truth is properly understood, the fact that it is true is supposedly self-evident or, since some allegedly necessary truths are very complicated, can be established on the basis of reasoning which proceeds entirely from self-evident truths. In this category different philosophers have at times placed the propositions of logic and mathematics, propositions asserting the existence of God, space and time, and purely conceptual claims, such as 'all men are male'. In the opposite contingent category were held to fall all the claims of history and science, such as 'Caesar crossed the Rubicon' and 'Paraquat kills plants'. Such propositions can be fully understood by someone who doubts their truth, and even if we are sure that they are true, we are able to envisage circumstances in which they are not or might not have been true.

Most philosophers are now ready to accept that this distinction was originally drawn too sharply and that it is an error to suppose that all propositions can be neatly assigned to one category or the other. Nevertheless the distinction remains useful as a rough and ready expository tool. Political claims, we may assert, are about the world as we experience it and perhaps about how it ought to be. They are certainly not themselves claims or inferences from claims which have only to be understood in order to be believed. In short they are all contingent.

Subjectivity and Objectivity

There is a further rough and ready distinction that may be drawn between different propositions within the contingent category. This further distinction is between what I shall label *subjective* and *objective* propositions. Although these terms are in common use, they are not always used in exactly the same way, so it is necessary to specify how they are employed here. Statements like 'Jane has a headache' and 'George likes veal' are to be understood as subjective. They contrast with such objective statements as 'Oswald killed Kennedy' and 'All dinosaurs died before the last Ice Age'.

Subjective statements involve claims whose truth is primarily a function of the consciousness of particular individuals and it is not normally profitable for us to engage in argument about them. So in the case of Jane's alleged headache and George's professed partiality to veal, we can attempt to make an inference based on Jane or George's observed behaviour if we distrust or do not have access to their own testimonies, but this will always be second-best. The best evidence we can obtain is an honest report from Jane or George, and it should be noted that *their* views are not the outcome of any process of reasoning.

Objective statements by contrast are ones whose truth is dependent on at least one factor which is independent of the consciousness of particular individuals. Whether it is true that the dinosaurs all died before the last Ice Age depends on what actually happened, not on what we make of the evidence. Some statements may be dependent on factors of both kinds. 'I see a man running on the grassy knoll' is a claim whose truth depends both on whether there really is such a man and also on my own perceptions. If there is in fact no man running on the grassy knoll, the claim 'I see a man running on the grassy knoll' is false, although the subective statement 'I think I see a man running on the grassy knoll' may still be true. I shall choose to treat such claims as objective because their content includes an element which is worth arguing about.

The difference between objective and subjective statements is apparent when we reflect on the circumstances in which we might doubt whether a proposition is true. In the case of objective statements, we are aware of the possibility of error even in relation to the kind of claims of which we are most confident. Thus however sure I am that I see a man running on the grassy knoll, there is the possibility that I am mistaken, because for example what I see may really be a woman or I am taken in by a trick of the light or I have had too much to drink. By contrast it is only in very special circumstances that we can entertain doubts that relate to subjective claims about ourselves. Taking the above examples Jane or George can themselves be in doubt only in the most unusual circumstances. They may perhaps be uncertain about their grasp of English, but then their problem is merely conceptual. Or they might have threshold doubts. Jane might be unsure whether a slight discomfort is sufficient to count as a headache, and George may wonder whether his attitude to veal is quite positive enough to constitute liking it. Here again the problem is conceptual. Jane and George know what they have experienced but are uncertain about how to describe it. We have already seen that it is quite appropriate for many concepts to accommodate a degree of fuzziness, so we should not attach too much significance to this kind of difficulty. The question of whether a slight twinge really is a headache is not a question that must always have a clear answer, any more than there must always be a clear answer at dawn or dusk to the question of whether it is day-time or nighttime. Finally Jane and George may simply have been insufficiently attentive, or, in George's case, have inadequate recall of the experience. Maybe Jane is just waking up, but still thinks she might only be dreaming that she has a headache. Maybe George simply cannot remember for sure if and when he has ever had veal, or how it tasted. However if Jane is given just a little more time, and George is fed some veal, these uncertainties will disappear. In standard cases there is no room for error in subjective judgements.

That it is futile to engage in rational argument in order to settle questions about an individual's experiences will be widely accepted for it is a truism that no-one can suffer someone else's pain or share in someone else's sensations. It may be thought however that there is more of a problem when we consider statements which are apparently objective in form, but which seem to be reducible to the subjective. So if George says 'Veal is nice' and Jane says 'Veal is horrible' it sounds as if there is a genuine disagreement between them, rather than a mere difference in taste. But do we really think that George and Jane are committed to holding that the other is mistaken about something? If we conclude that each statement is in fact reducible to an expression of the speaker's own taste, then we see that there is little scope for rational argument, and that what is expressed is a mere difference rather than a disagreement. Their different attitudes to veal no more constitute a disagreement between them than does the fact that George is male and Jane is female.

Consider next a more difficult case, namely that of religious statements. Here the important question is whether religious belief rests upon reason or faith. Medieval theologians, such as St Augustine, thought that many religious truths were accessible to reason and offered 'proofs' of God's existence. If this view of religion is correct then statements of religious belief are objective. Most modern believers however do not imagine that the case for God's existence is such that those who deny it can be convicted of a defect of rationality, but instead assert that it is a matter of faith. However, although their belief is thus based on their own experiences and inner certainty, the certainty is generally about something which is claimed to be external. The difference here is comparable to that between saying, as one wakes up, 'God spoke to me in my dream', which is a believer's statement and makes an objective claim, and 'I dreamed that God spoke to me' which is a subjective claim that might be made even by an atheist. Sometimes however those who describe themselves as believers may merely assert propositions like 'God exists for me'. It would be out of place here to analyse what exactly this might mean, but if it implies that although non-believers may be missing out on something they are not actually in error, then it is to be taken as a subjective claim.

I have thought it worthwhile to take some time to use non-political examples to illustrate what I take to be the difference between objective and subjective questions because I have often found that students tell me that political questions are subjective, by which they mean that each of us has our own standpoint that cannot be touched by rational debate. This view incidentally is to be sharply distinguished from *relativism*. When applied to political questions, the relativist holds that there are no universally appropriate answers, but only ones which hold within a particular community. I shall return to relativism in chapter 16, but for the moment we should merely note that it is a doctrine about the limits of rational argument, and unlike subjectivism does not entail the view that rational argument is pointless. If subjectivism is true, then apparently conflicting political judgements are all reducible to expressions of different peoples' basic wants. By basic wants I mean those wants which people have for their own sake, as opposed to those wants whose satisfaction is desired as instrumental to the satisfaction of other wants. This point needs to be made because instrumental wants are the outcome of a process of reasoning. If I want to go to the dentist because I believe that she has relevant skill which she is ready to deploy to alleviate my toothache, this is an instrumental want which I have good reason to abandon if I am given reliable information to the effect that she is always drunk, although my basic want to be free of toothache will remain. Similarly if I wish to live in peace, there is still room for argument about whether this desire is more likely to be satisfied by the election of a government committed to disarmament rather than one committed to high military expenditure.

To conclude that political opinions are subjective in status or ultimately reducible to the subjective is to take a debunking view of politics in that it is hard to see how one can believe such a view to be true and still in good faith engage in political argument. The analogy is with the parallel analysis of religious utterances. If a believer asserts that 'God spoke to me in my dream' but takes the meaning of this proposition to be reducible to 'I dreamed that God spoke to me', she could scarcely expect her assertion to cut much ice with non-believers. 'So what?' is the predictable response. Similarly if political claims are merely a way of voicing demands based on our own wants, there seems little point in making them. Thus if the assertion that 'University staff ought be exempted from income tax liability' is no more than an expression of the yearning of academics for such a measure it is hard to see how they could expect it to cut any ice with those who would have to pay more tax in order to enable university staff to pay none.

The acceptance of a subjective analysis would make a big difference to political argument as normally conducted. The reason is that we should have to abandon the assumption that consistency is important, since it has no application in the subjective realm. Suppose I like strawberries, raspberries and gooseberries, as well as strawberry and raspberry fool, but I do not like gooseberry fool. If someone asks how it is that I don't like gooseberry fool when I like all these other fruits and desserts, I can with perfect propriety say, 'Perhaps it is surprising but there it is; I don't have to reconcile my dislike of gooseberry fool with my liking for the others.' Similarly I may agree that I did like gooseberry fool last year or last week or yesterday, but I may still maintain that I don't like it now. This contrasts with what is normally assumed to be true of political beliefs. If for example I used to but have now ceased to oppose paying ransom to secure the release of hostages, I would normally be expected to explain either that there has been a relevant change in the circumstances, or that I now believe that I was wrong in the past. What I cannot claim within the normally accepted canons of political discussion is 'I know I said something else last time but I just happen to feel differently about it now from how I felt then.'

The reality of political argument is then that consistency is taken to be important. The charge that what a government minister is saying now is different from what he said in opposition or before he was elected is part of the common currency of almost any Parliamentary debate or election campaign. Indeed the opinions of a particular politician or any person with political commitments often bear a relationship to one another which is considerably closer than mere consistency. This I have sometimes demonstrated by asking a class of students for their opinions on particular questions of home and foreign policy. My experience has been that those who are in favour of high expenditure on social welfare at home are more likely than other members of the class to be sympathetic to third world aid, and less likely to favour capital punishment for convicted murderers. Strictly speaking of course no individual's position on any one of these three issues is entailed by his view of either of the others. Indeed history has thrown up some notable examples of political leaders such as Mussolini who have combined the pursuit of social welfare at home with overseas policies that have shown scant regard for the welfare of foreigners. But most of our political attitudes proceed from a relatively small number of guiding principles. If we have already thought about one set of problems, we are quite likely to find that we favour principles which seem applicable to other problems. So for example it is no surprise if those who have already thought a great deal about abortion are likely to find it easier to address themselves to a 'new' issue such as surrogate motherhood. Another way of putting this is to say that in the political opinions of most people we can observe what can be called *ideological connectedness*. The position of the eclectic who contemplates every issue on its own merits may not be impossible, but it is daunting. The problem is that he must always struggle to find a basis for deliberating about a 'new' problem and, because his views are not based on a small number of guiding principles, it is much more likely that his opinion on one question will be at variance with his opinion on others. How for example can the eclectic have a defensible position on budgetary strategy if each proposal to spend government money is to be considered in isolation? Ideological connectedness is what enables us to make generalizations about people being 'left-wing' or 'right-wing' and helps to guide us in the direction of a consistent set of opinions.

If we conclude that the debunking subjectivist analysis is correct, the consequence is gloomy. In general it does not matter greatly if we have unresolvable differences about the food we like or the paintings we appreciate, because, although there are some who feel challenged or affronted by other people's likes and dislikes, for the most part we simply go our own way. Indeed life for many would be less agreeable if everyone they encountered had the same tastes and liked the same things. However in politics such a relaxed view of difference is impossible, because other people's preferences have a significant impact on our own lives. Thus if I want the benefits of cheap nuclear power and you want an environment free of all nuclear waste, we cannot simply agree to differ, since our preferences are, at any rate in the present state of technology, incompatible. But if rational argument about politics is possible, there is the chance that one of us may convince the other. And even if we fail to reach agreement on the substance of the question, there is at least the possibility that such argument may lead to agreement on what is an appropriate procedure, for example a vote of all adult citizens or by elected representatives, for determining which view will for the time being prevail. But if rational argument even about procedure is impossible, then our alternatives, when confronted with demands that are incompatible with our own, are to capitulate, to fight or to compromise. Politics, on this view, can never be anything but an unending power struggle and we delude ourselves if we think otherwise.

Nothing I have said so far demonstrates that this picture is not the correct one. What I claim is firstly that politics in fact proceeds on the assumption that rational argument is relevant and secondly that the outlook is gloomy if this assumption is false. But outlooks sometimes are gloomy. In order to try to determine whether this is so, we need to look at political argument in practice.

6

Ideology and Justification

We noted in chapter 5 that political differences are normally presumed to represent not just differences in attitude but real disagreements in belief. From the perspective of a person with political convictions, anyone who holds different beliefs is liable to be seen as mistaken; activists with different beliefs are viewed as opponents and sometimes as enemies. But if we have clear political convictions, how can we hope to justify our own beliefs and demonstrate the errors of our opponents? Does not the persistence of political differences suggest that such a task must be impossible?

To these questions there are no short answers. We shall just have to look at how those who adopt quite different approaches, such as liberals, conservatives and socialists, seek to justify their conclusions. In order to designate these different approaches I shall use the familiar label, *ideologies*. We have already noted the phenomenon of ideological connectedness, which enables us to trace out a certain pattern in the thinking of most politically interested individuals. If we embrace an ideology, then, as noted in chapter 5, we have the advantage of a basis for thinking about new problems. But how are we to decide whether we are liberals, conservatives, socialists or whatever? Initially at least the business of acquiring political opinions is not the outcome of a project of rational enquiry, but something that happens as a result of our experience and the influence that others have on us.

That political beliefs may in fact be generated as a result of socialization makes them not special but typical. Consider for example beliefs about scientific matters. My belief that the speed of light is approximately 186,000 miles per second was not acquired as a result of any research that I did, nor indeed of my familiarity with the experimental work of others. It was what I was told in a school, which my parents determined I should attend, by a teacher I trusted, and it was what I read in books that he told me to read. But my parents' decision and my encounter with this teacher and those books were not matters of chance. My school was supported by public funds and was staffed by teachers who were university graduates. I was being prepared for examinations which were to be marked by other graduates of these same universities. No teacher would have lasted long if he had taught his pupils that there were no such things as light waves. The school was subject to periodic inspection by servants of the state, who would have reported adversely if they perceived that an idiosyncratic physics curriculum was being pursued. The texts I consulted were produced by educational publishers who would have gone bankrupt if they published books that denied the received wisdom. The universities from which the authors of the physics textbooks graduated have always sought to appoint staff who will be well thought of by scholars in other universities. So my parents' decisions and my own encounters with teachers and books were typical of the decisions of other parents and the encounters of other children. Moreover having abandoned physics early in my school career, I never subsequently sought to verify my belief about the speed of light. I know that this belief fits in well with other things that I have heard physicists say and with the results of some famous experiments to which I have heard them refer, and though I lack the knowledge to measure the speed of light for myself, academic life has brought me into contact with many of those who are generally regarded as competent to do it and to explain how it is done. Meeting them has reinforced both my confidence that beliefs which are universal amongst academic scientists are much more likely to be right than wrong and my acceptance of the readiness with which parents speak with apparent authority on a wide range of subjects. I have therefore been ready to answer my children's questions about such matters as the speed of light.

That such beliefs are often socially generated does not however mean that rational justification is unimportant. My confidence in my belief about the speed of light is not based simply on the fact that I have discovered it to be the prevailing orthodoxy. If that was all, I should have to consider the possibility that it is simply a product of the fact that I live in a society of conformists. No doubt public recognition of the inadequacy of our science, even if well-merited, would be as difficult to secure as the recognition that the emperor has no clothes. But just as emperors are on occasion naked, so it is conceivable that science does not deserve the public respect it is normally accorded. However my confidence reflects not only my perception that the experts agree but also that this consensus about the speed of light extends to the method of testing it. Indeed we would not describe someone as a scientist unless we thought that she had some idea as to how her scientific beliefs could be justified.

Similarly I cannot expect others to take my political assertions seriously if I have no idea how to justify them. In politics we do not have the excuse that we require highly specialized abilities or expensive equipment to handle the justifying arguments or evidence. So those with serious political commitments are expected to say something themselves in support of their beliefs. In order to justify their beliefs, they need to show that it is rational to adopt them. So let us define an ideology as *any systematic approach to politics which purports to offer a rational basis for determining the proper outcome of all or most of the issues of the day*.

The number of distinct ideologies that are encountered in Western societies is small. This is explained by the fact that ideologies are socially generated, and Western societies have broadly similar social and economic structures. We shall be considering liberalism, conservatism and socialism. I do not mean to suggest that these are the only three ideological possibilities, or that I shall consider every variant of the three, or even that the total number of ideologies is something which can be precisely quantified. Since Western societies are all pluralist and open to ideas that emanate from other cultures, it is a mistake to seek to define precise boundaries between each tradition of political thought. We are not like colonial administrators drawing lines on maps. Our object is simply to adopt a classification of convenience, which will enable us to come to terms with the arguments most frequently encountered in political debate, rather than to divide the world of political ideas into different 'isms', each of which is regarded as representing a monolithic corpus of belief to be defended by any true adherent. So we should not for example assume that if public ownership of the means of production is taken to be a characteristic strand of socialist ideology, it must be endorsed by all socialists, or that professing socialists who fail to adopt this position are traitors to the cause. Equally we must not exclude the possibility that some non-socialists might support the public ownership of particular industries.

There is another reason why we need to be cautious about the use of labels such as 'conservative', 'liberal' and 'socialist'. These terms are frequently deployed simply as descriptions for the pro-gramme and supporters of particular political parties. In Britain the term *conservative* might thus be thought of as applying to all those who support the Conservative Party. This can lead to confusion because the name of a political party often reflects the desire of its founders or current leaders to lay claim to some particular tradition of political thought. So the reason why a given party bears a given name may be historical or even tactical rather than ideological. Thus we find that many of the attitudes of supporters of the Liberal Party of Australia are similar to those of supporters of the Conservative Party in Britain. In any case politicians and Party establishments always temper ideology with pragmatism. So the Labour Government of Mr David Lange in New Zealand, regarded as socialist in that the New Zealand Labour Party is a member of the Socialist International, claimed credit for having reduced economic protectionism and for having withdrawn subsidies from New Zealand's own agriculture and industry.[1] In order to avoid confusion, I shall use capital letters where I am using a term in a way that simply reflects a Party label. Thus it is beyond question that Mrs Thatcher was at the head of Conservative governments in Britain from 1979 until 1990, but this fact does not entail that she was a faithful upholder of conservative principles. However even though it is no part of my purpose to define the ideological positions of Mr Lange or Mrs Thatcher or of any particular politician, it would be absurd to write about political argument without referring to actual examples. So in talking of the three 'isms', I shall refer to practical examples of liberal, conservative and socialist policies, but readers are asked to bear in mind that even the most ideological of politicians are likely to make pragmatic compromises so that their arguments and actions at best only approximate to an underlying ideological position.

One final qualification to our discussion of the 'isms' relates to the purpose of this book. I shall not be seeking to give the comprehensive account of each that would be appropriate to a study in the history of ideas. Nor am I seeking to engage in a systematic analysis of the strengths and weaknesses of any of them. My purpose in examining each ideology is to say enough about each one so as to give an indication of the possibility of engaging in rational argument about its merits or demerits. Because conservatives allow a somewhat inconspicuous role for rational argument, I have less to say about conservatism than about liberalism and socialism. But even in the case of conservatism, I shall suggest that rational argument about its merits is not unimportant. Ultimately I shall be seeking to use my discussion of liberalism, conservatism and socialism to draw a conclusion about the extent to which rational argument about politics is feasible.

Further Reading

The importance of conceptual analysis and definition is discussed in D. D. Raphael, *Problems of Political Philosophy*, 2nd edn, (London: Macmillan, 1990) and D. Miller, 'Linguistic philosophy and political theory' in *The Nature of Political Theory*, ed. D. Miller and L. Siedentop (Oxford University Press, 1984). A basic puzzle about how our concepts succeed in having any meaning at all is briefly outlined in chapter 5 of T. Nagel's short introduction to philosophy, *What Does It All Mean?* (Oxford University Press, 1987). A famous challenge to the alleged impossibility of obtaining an evaluative conclusion from a factual premise is J. R. Searle, 'How to derive "ought" from "is"' in *Theories of Ethics*, ed. P. Foot (Oxford University Press, 1967). Also in the same volume and on the question of the relationship between facts and values, see P.

Foot, 'Moral beliefs'. The issue of subjectivity versus objectivity is discussed in the context of moral values in J. L. Mackie, *Ethics* (Harmondsworth: Penguin Books, 1977), chapter 1, and in R. Dworkin, *A Matter of Principle* (Oxford University Press, 1985), chapter 7. It is related to what is seen as a problem emerging in different areas of philosophy in T. Nagel, *Mortal Questions* (Cambridge University Press, 1979), chapter 14.

There are many books on political ideologies. Some feature an introductory discussion of the nature of ideology followed by one or two chapters on each of the predominant 'isms'. B. Goodwin, *Using Political Ideas* (London: Duckworth, 1982) and G. Graham, *Politics in its Place* (Oxford University Press, 1986) are, from a philosopher's viewpoint, the best examples. Some books which focus on particular ideologies are mentioned at the end of Parts Two, Three and Four.

Part II
Liberalism

7

Economic Liberalism

The history of liberalism in the English-speaking world may appear curiously broken-backed. In the eighteenth and nineteenth centuries, much of the thrust of liberalism centred on an assertion of the rights of individuals to determine their own destiny and an insistence that the responsibilities of government did not go beyond the provision of a framework for the exercise of these rights. These ideas have their roots in sources such as Locke's *Two Treatises of Government*, published in 1690, and Adam Smith's *Wealth of Nations*, published in 1776.[1] Among practical politicians, the centrality of rights was asserted in the United States by Jefferson and Madison, and the restricted view of the role of government was given expression in the commitment to *laissez-faire* economics promoted in nineteenth century England by Cobden, Bright and the Manchester School of Liberals.

During the first half of the twentieth century, however, liberalism came to be perceived as having a strong commitment to the introduction of the welfare state. This was especially marked in Britain where the foundations had been laid by Lloyd George as Chancellor of the Exchequer in the Liberal Government elected in 1908, and where the expansion of welfare provision by the Labour Government of 1945 leaned heavily on plans drawn up by the distinguished Liberal economist, and latterly Member of Parliament, William Beveridge. In the United States, liberals backed Franklin D. Roosevelt's New Deal which from 1933 introduced social welfare legislation and sought to counter the effects of the Depression by involving the government directly in such projects as the development of the Tennessee Valley. None of these policies was intended as an implementation of any particular work of political theory, but all of them can be seen as justified in terms of Hobhouse's influential book, *Liberalism*,[2] which in the early years of the twentieth century had argued in favour of the idea that the state's concerns should include the distribution of wealth. A more recent and complex attempt to provide a theoretical framework for the more interventionist kind of liberalism was that of Rawls's *A Theory of Justice*. I shall call these two approaches *economic* and *welfare liberalism*, though it should be noted that each of them represents a view of the proper role of government, and not merely a set of opinions on economic or welfare policy. These conceptions of liberalism are sharply different from one another, for precisely those policies which are at the heart of welfare liberalism represent a clear breach of the *laissez-faire* approach.

As a result of the politics of recent years, no-one can possibly suppose that welfare liberalism has supplanted economic liberalism. At the end of the 1980s it seemed almost as if the reverse was the case, in that governments committed to welfare liberalism had virtually disappeared from the Western world. The decision of the British Liberal Party in 1988 to wind itself up in favour of a broad centrist grouping may be seen as one indication of the decline of this form of liberalism. Economic liberalism on the other hand was alive and well not only in the theories of such writers as Hayek and Nozick, but also in the deeds of politicians like President Reagan and Mrs Thatcher. This was only superficially obscured by the fact that for many years in both Britain and America the use of the term *liberal* was usually associated with welfare liberalism so that those whom I describe as economic liberals often prefer to see themselves as 'conservatives'. In Britain those who hold such views have usually, like Mrs Thatcher, been members of the Conservative Party.

The example of Mrs Thatcher was particularly interesting. What was unusual about 'Thatcherism' was the extent to which its policies were shaped by those with a conscious interest in ideology. Although, to judge from her speeches, there is no reason to think that Mrs Thatcher herself ever devoted much time to theoretical contemplation, her approach to government was strongly influenced by her close colleague, Sir Keith Joseph, with whom she was involved in the establishment of the Centre for Policy Studies, the so-called Thatcherite Think Tank, in 1974.[3] Joseph had been a minister in earlier Conservative administrations when he had displayed a strong commitment to the welfare state and the mixed economy. However during a period out of office in the 1970s he became converted to the ideas of such writers as Hayek and Friedman and concluded that his previous position had been indistinguishable from socialism.[4] Mrs Thatcher herself spoke with warm approval of Adam Smith and was regarded by some as a modern version of a nineteenth-century liberal.[5] Although some would argue that Mrs Thatcher's opinions on social issues contained strong elements of traditional conservatism, I think it reasonable to treat 'Thatcherism' as a version of economic liberalism. Whilst the striking difference between the two varieties of liberalism has already been remarked upon, I shall also seek to bring out an important similarity, namely their commitment to individualism.

Economic Liberalism and the Individual

Consider some statements made by practising politicians. The first was by Ronald Reagan just prior to his election as President in 1980.

> I believe we can embark on a new age of reform . . . and an era of national renewal . . . that will make government responsible again to people, that will revitalize the values of family, work and neighbourhood and that will restore our private and independent social institutions. These institutions always have served as buffer and bridge between the individual and the state – and these institutions, not government are the real sources of our economic and social progress as a people. That's why . . . we must control . . . the growth of Federal spending, (why) we must reduce tax rates to stimulate work and savings and investment.[6]

In 1980 Mrs Thatcher described her objectives in these terms.

Individuals will have a fair chance, by their own efforts, of winning
happiness and security for themselves and their children and, in
the process, enlarging the wealth and strength of their country.[7]

John Howard, Leader of the Australian Liberal Party, struck a
similar note in the course of the 1987 Federal Election.

The important thing is lower taxation will provide greater incentive
for everyone to work harder. That helps our businesses produce
more and thus lift our productivity as a nation. That's the way
out. That's what this election is all about: lower tax and the
incentive to achieve a better and more prosperous life for yourself
and your family – the incentive to get in front again.[8]

All of these statements indicate a clear view of the role of government. But any view of how a community ought to be governed
must be backed up by a conception of what constitutes a good
life for its members. Are there any indications in these political
statements of such a conception?

What these three politicians assert is the need for the role of
government to be limited. In terms of foreign policy, leaders such
as President Reagan and Mrs Thatcher always placed stress on
human rights. But the rights for which they spoke up were almost
always the rights which were denied throughout Eastern Europe
prior to the advent to power of President Gorbachev. These were
the rights to participate in the political process or to freedom of
movement and opinion and worship. Little mention if any was
made to rights of employment and subsistence. All of the politicians we have cited accept that governments must spend money
on providing internal security and defence, but that otherwise
government activity must be reined in so as to keep taxes low. So
for example the Thatcher government discontinued subsidies to
businesses that could not pay their way, privatized industries that
were publicly owned, and reduced expenditure on education and
social services. The proffered justification was not only on the
ground of efficiency but also on the ground that public expenditure in these areas leads to high taxation.

Why is low taxation important? The reason is that the role of
government is seen as an enabling one. So long as government

provides a secure framework which gives enterprising individuals the opportunity to do as well as they can for themselves and their families, it has done all that the economic liberal thinks can be expected of it. To allow a more ambitious role for the state is to give unjustified power to bureaucrats and to assume, as it is put in Britain, that the man from Whitehall knows best. What is sometimes disparagingly called the 'nanny state' creates a dependency culture so that citizens do not seek to use their initiative to better themselves.

The Importance of Choice

What makes a person's position *better*? What is the good life? These are not issues on which economic liberals must be neutral, but they are questions which they believe that individuals should in large measure be permitted to settle for themselves. But no meaningful choice can be made unless there is a range of options available. For this reason economic liberals attach importance to the individual's ability to attain material prosperity. Wealth is not necessarily seen as good in itself, but it is of instrumental value in that its possession enhances the range of available choices. The economic liberal does not deny that there are significant ethical questions about how the individual uses his wealth, but subject only to the need to respect the freedom of others, these are held to be ones for the individual himself to decide. Addressing the General Assembly of the Church of Scotland, Mrs Thatcher declared, 'It is not the creation of wealth that is wrong, but love of money for its own sake. The spiritual dimension comes in deciding what one does with the wealth'.[9]

What government can contribute, from the perspective of the economic liberal, is a framework that makes it possible for citizens to acquire wealth by their own efforts and which ensures that individual freedom is respected. Low taxation is thought to enhance choice in two ways. Apart from the obvious advantages of such a policy for the more enterprising, economic liberals believe that the policy will also have benefits for those who are less enterprising, in that they will enjoy employment opportunities and options for consumer goods and leisure activities which are generated by the enterprise of their fellow-citizens. We should here notice an assumption about human nature in that it seems to be taken for granted that people will always be motivated by the prospect of becoming richer. For if this assumption were false and there proved to be a point at which people were satisfied with their material wealth, the effect of a low rate of tax would presumably be to ensure that the more enterprising reached this point more quickly and so did less work. This would then result in a loss of opportunities for the less enterprising.

Economic Liberalism and Individualism

These familiar themes of economic liberalism, echoed by the politicians we have quoted, are all to be found in such earlier theorists as Locke and Smith as well as contemporary writers like Hayek and Nozick. I have already remarked on one traditional liberal theme, namely the commitment to *individualism*. One of the difficulties with this term,[10] as with others like *ideology* and *community*, is that different writers use it in different ways. As used here, individualism is the view that it is for each citizen to determine and pursue his own good. By contrast communitarianism is the view that the good of all citizens is the common concern of all citizens. Both of these stances can be held in more or less extreme ways so that we can think in terms of a spectrum. At one end are extreme individualists who believe that there are no questions which should properly be determined by the community and thus no proper role for the state at all, and that individuals are thus sovereign in regulating their own lives. At the other end are extreme communitarians who believe that the community should regulate everything, from religious worship to sexual behaviour, so that all activity is either compulsory or forbidden. Most people of course occupy neither of these positions and wish some questions to be left to the community and others to the individual. As I use the terms, whether someone is to be counted as an individualist or a communitarian is a function of the end of the spectrum to which they are closer.

The political assertions quoted above are individualist, because they advocate a form of government in which individuals are, with suitable qualifications, expected to look after themselves. A celebrated contemporary endorsement of this position was Mrs Thatcher's assertion that there are no such things as societies, only individuals and families.[11] The reference to families makes clear that she is close to, but does not embrace the extreme individualist thesis that a community is nothing more than an aggregation of people who choose to live in some form of association with one another. On this view talk about the good or interests of a community would only have meaning to the extent that it is *reducible* to talk about the good or interests of particular individuals. So 'social justice' may be rejected as a meaningless phrase, unless it can be reduced to talk about the just treatment of individuals.

The Individualism of John Locke

Political individualism reflects a view of human motivation. If the members of a community are viewed as sovereign individuals, their readiness to live in political association with one another presumably depends on their seeing it as advantageous for them to do so. But is it clear that it is always advantageous? John Locke (1632–1704) is the first significant liberal individualist to grapple with this question. The first thoroughgoing masterpiece of individualism was however Thomas Hobbes's *Leviathan*, published in 1651. Hobbes thought that the good life consisted in 'commodious living',[12] which, put more crudely, means getting as much as possible of what one likes. But he saw that if we all engaged in the unconstrained pursuit of self-interest, none of us would be likely to have much success in attaining it. Total freedom would mean mutual destruction and chaos. The problem is that we tend to want the same things as one another and in a world of limited resources our different self-interests collide. In consequence no-one can trust anyone else and life is 'solitary, poor, nasty, brutish and short'.[13] His solution was however authoritarian rather than liberal. Hobbes thought that for each subject the pursuit of self-interest had to be constrained by acceptance of a virtually unconditional duty to do whatever the sovereign, or political leader, required.

Locke's liberal individualism has its roots in the rejection of this authoritarian solution. He thought that what stands between us and the ability to get the things we want is not simply the danger of being attacked by belligerent neighbours and the threat of chaos and anarchy, but also the menace of autocratic and arbitrary power. Government was seen as justified only if it derived its authority from the consent of the citizens. Its function was to enable people to determine the course of their own lives. Each individual, thought Locke, was a rational agent and endowed with God-given natural rights to life, liberty and property; similarly each was bound by a duty to respect these rights in others. Since individuals cannot in isolation act effectively in defence of these rights, it was rational, Locke supposed, where others were similarly minded, for each person to abandon his own freedom to act in his own defence in favour of a state which would act to secure the natural rights of all. It is important to notice that Lockean citizens did not abandon their natural rights, but only their freedom to act against others in order to secure these rights. Equally the government which exercised this freedom on their behalf did not acquire any rights over others which each citizen did not already have as an individual. So governments remained under a duty to respect the natural rights of all.

The Lockean answer to our question about the good life thus involves the pursuit of self-interest but constrained for each person by the recognition that others must be accorded freedom to pursue *their* self-interest. It is important to realize that our duties in respect of the natural rights of others are largely negative. In Locke's view natural law imposes on me a duty not to impede others in the enjoyment of their life, liberty and property; I am not however required to forgo any advantage or spend any of my time or energy in order to ensure that they have much in the way of life, liberty and property to enjoy.

The picture this suggests is that the only duties we have to others are those of natural law and those that we voluntarily take on ourselves. In fact Locke does not conceive of human beings as being quite so solitary. He departs from extreme individualism, in the direction followed by Mrs Thatcher, in taking the family to be a natural unit rather than the product of an agreement based on rational self-interest. It should also be noted that Locke's view does not preclude an individual from choosing to devote himself to the welfare of others or entering into positive commitments to look after them. The point is that no-one is bound to provide positive help to others save by his own choice; because Lockean rights are negative in character, a state which used public funds to seek to alleviate poverty would lack the authority to do so. In other words Lockean rights are similar to the kinds of right which figured in the foreign policy speeches of politicians such as President Reagan and Mrs Thatcher most especially when denouncing Soviet leaders of the pre-Gorbachev era.

Economic Liberalism and Rights

The suppositions that the individual's basic rights are God-given or exactly as Locke characterized them were not enduring features of liberalism. What characterized economic liberalism however was the conviction that it is for the rational individual, just so long as he respects similar freedom for others, to make what he wills of his life. What is distinctive is the combination of reason and individualism. The good life for the individual citizen consists in using his own judgement about what to believe and to do. In order to put his judgements into effect, he must acquire the resources that enable him to shape his own life. The requirement that such freedom be equal for all sets a limit on the degree of self-determination that is possible. Individuals clearly cannot all be free to choose their own political arrangements. But what the liberal can insist on is accountability or the importance of these arrangements reflecting the desires and choices of all who are to be subject to them.

How can this be done when people do not all want the same things as one another? The traditional liberal solution is majority government provided that there are safeguards for minorities. These safeguards usually take the form of legally enforcible rights, such as those entrenched in the US Constitution or upheld by the European Court of Human Rights. What characterizes such rights is that they are rights to be allowed to participate in the political process or rights to be left alone or rights not be discriminated against. They are not rights to be provided with resources or services.

A general observation to be made here about economic liberals is that typically they follow Locke in placing great emphasis on rights. Because they think of each individual as endowed with personal sovereignty, that of government is always seen as constrained by the limits of the authority which the individual citizens can be held to have vested in it. Since this personal sovereignty is something which belongs to *each* individual, there can in principle be no justification for anyone being subjected against his or her will to the authority of a state, even where this state enjoys overwhelming support.

Such a principle is open to being interpreted in a way that entirely eliminates the possibility of effective government. In practice liberals are not anarchists. What Locke required was the consent of everyone to the constitution in terms of which decisions are made, rather than universal consent to each law, policy or political appointment. Even so he was driven onto some notoriously shaky ground in his account of what constitutes consenting to the authority of the state,[14] and he did not think that dissenters had the right to stand their ground and defy authority. Whilst they choose to live within a community, they must abide by the law provided that their basic rights are not denied. But the basic right to liberty means that those who do not wish to accept the authority of the state must be permitted to leave. In practice the value of this right to a dissenter depends on the willingness of another community to accept him, and on his own readiness to live elsewhere, so that being permitted to leave does not necessarily make departure a live option.

The difficulties or compromises that may be involved in the application of liberal principles should not obscure the nature of the characteristically liberal appeal to rights. It should be noted that the appeal invokes moral, not merely legal, rights. A test of whether someone conceives of rights in this way is whether he believes that the law will on occasion need to be changed *in order to* give effect to rights. For example some argue that the law must recognize the right of an adopted child to know the identity of her natural parents. Plainly if the law is supposed to *recognize* a right, there must be some pre-legal sense in which that right is already held to exist.

However it is not only liberals who believe in moral rights. We are often inclined to describe any benefit or opportunity which we think that people morally ought to have as being their right. For example we can imagine a member of the Polish Communist Party who in the days when Poland was still a one-party state might have asserted that his Catholic fellow-citizens had a moral right to attend Mass. By this he might have meant no more than that any attempt to interfere with worship would have been wrong because it would have been so greatly resented as to lead to the likely destabilization of the state. In this case the communist does indeed believe in the right to attend Mass, but his belief is based on his estimate of the likely consequences of any attempt to deny this right. He is thus operating with a subordinate conception of moral rights. His reasons are such that he would be happy to abandon his support for the right of worship in changed circumstances. So if for example he thought that the Church had lost popularity and that public opinion might be ready to accept the change, he could be expected no longer to be voicing support for the right to attend Mass.

In contrast to the view of our hypothetical Polish communist, rights, as liberals have traditionally conceived of them, are fundamental rather than subordinate. Someone who believes in freedom of religion as a fundamental right thinks that preventing people from attending Mass is wrong *in itself* and an injustice to those who wish to attend, even in circumstances in which the wider ramifications of preventing people from engaging in religious observance might be good. I do not mean to suggest that all liberals are so uncompromising in their support for fundamental rights as to believe that these must be upheld however catastrophic the cost of doing so. One can imagine that many who adopt a rights-centred approach will concede that they can be suspended in circumstances of war or great necessity. The test of whether someone should still be regarded as an upholder of fundamental rights is a function of how unusual are the circumstances in which he is ready to contemplate suspension and whether he recognizes that such suspension, *even where justified,* does involve injustice so that the right does not disappear without trace. This may seem puzzling, but it is possible to suspend rights *in extremis* whilst recognizing a commitment to compensate those whose rights have been overridden as soon as this becomes feasible.

In all cases, however, the appeal to fundamental moral rights takes priority over social objectives which are viewed merely as worthwhile. So those who believe in a fundamental right of worship can be expected to support the existence and enforcement of a corresponding legal right. If however the law does not permit freedom of worship or the government does nothing to ensure that such freedom is a reality, the person who asserts the existence of a fundamental moral right is committed to the view that the right remains. It is simply that the state infringes rather than protects it. Fundamental moral rights cannot, in the opinion of those who assert them, be set aside by government even with the support of the majority and in ordinary circumstances, when there is no war or similar emergency, they may be viewed in the phrase of the contemporary liberal theorist, Ronald Dworkin, as *trumping* other kinds of claim.[15]

Adam Smith and the Pursuit of Self-interest

We have seen that individualist philosophers like Hobbes and Locke take political institutions as developing in response to the way in which people pursue their own good. It has already been noted that modern economic liberals are committed to a motivational thesis, namely that people can be induced to be more productive by the prospect of economic gains for themselves and their families. Critics sometimes complain that liberal individualism endorses selfishness. Locke would certainly have regarded this as an unfair criticism of himself, because he maintained that there were limits to the amount of the world's resources that anyone was entitled to appropriate for himself.[16] He was however less interested in the distribution of wealth than in asserting man's natural rights and the constitutional arrangements needed to protect them.

The early liberal who was especially concerned with economics was Adam Smith. Smith took a similar line to Locke in his advocacy of a limited role for government. In 1776 he argued in *The Wealth of Nations* that the state must keep out of the creation and distribution of wealth. These matters, he thought, were best left to market forces which functioned as an Invisible Hand to shape the economy. It is worth quoting a part of Smith's famous description of this process.

> . . . man has almost constant occasion for the help of his brethren, and it is in vain for him to expect it from their benevolence only. He will be more likely to prevail if he can interest their self-love in his favour, and show them that it is for their own advantage to do for him what he requires of them. Whoever offers to another a bargain of any kind, proposes to do this. Give me that which I want, and you shall have this which you want, is the meaning of every such offer; and it is in this manner that we obtain from one another the far greater part of those good offices which we stand in need of. It is not from the benevolence of the butcher, the brewer, or the baker that we expect our dinner, but from their regard to their own interest. We address ourselves, not to their humanity but to their self-love . . .[17]

It is important to realize that Smith is not giving his moral approval to selfishness or even asserting the existence of a basic right for each person to pursue their self-interest independently of the ramifications for the community as a whole. In fact Smith believed that human beings were not solely occupied with the good of self and had a natural concern for the welfare of others. This is clear from the very first sentence of his earlier work, *The Theory of Moral Sentiments*.

How selfish soever man may be supposed, there are evidently some principles in his nature which interest him in the fortune of others, and render their happiness necessary to him, though he derives nothing from it except the pleasure of seeing it.[18]

But he was clear that man is always more keenly engaged in his own welfare than in the welfare of those around him, and with the cool realism of a social scientist observed that

The emotions of the spectator will still be very apt to fall short of the violence of what is felt by the sufferer. Mankind, though naturally sympathetic, never conceive, for what has befallen another, that degree of passion which naturally animates the person principally concerned.[19]

So Smith's assumption is that concern for others is real but subordinate to concern for self. It is other people's commitment to self-interest that gives us a reason for forming expectations of how they are likely to behave. Since they in turn have similar expectations about our own behaviour, we can cooperate more effectively with one another if we assume that everyone will pursue his self-interest than if we appeal to each other's real but weaker altruistic inclinations.

Smith can thus be seen as reinforcing Locke's view of the role of the state with a defence of the motivational thesis against the charge that it endorses undue selfishness. Moreover an acceptance of Smith's argument provides the economic liberal with the traditional response to the familiar objection that *laissez-faire* is a harsh prescription for the poor. The reality, Smith's argument asserts, is that although *laissez-faire* may not benefit all equally, it is in fact of benefit to all and not merely to the most enterprising, in that everyone is enabled to do as he wishes with a degree of assurance as to when he can expect to enlist the assistance of others.

Smith's argument thus complements Locke's attempt to found liberalism on an appeal to natural rights. Whereas Locke appealed to what he saw as justice for the individual, Smith argued that a liberal conception of government is in the common interest. Although this more pragmatic argument features less strongly in liberal rhetoric, both approaches are represented not only in the utterances of politicians but in the theorizing of contemporary economic liberals.

We remarked earlier that the theory of economic liberalism enjoyed a rebirth during the 1980s in the wake of the failures of many Western governments committed to high public spending. These failures led many economists to abandon the belief advanced by Keynes that public spending is the antidote to economic depression. There was a corresponding growth in the influence of economists like Milton Friedman who embraced a modern restatement of Smith's reliance on self-interest and market forces. I wish however to focus on two other theorists who have been influential in right-wing circles. Their writings are more philosophical in tone than those of Friedman and they respectively mirror the different emphases of Locke and Smith. They are Robert Nozick and Friedrich Hayek.

Modern Economic Liberalism: Nozick and Hayek

Nozick's statement of modern liberal theory adopts a starting point which is modelled on that of Locke. He assumes a state of nature which is prior to any political framework and which is populated by sovereign individuals with basic rights to life, liberty and property. These rights constitute constraints upon the freedom of action of others.[20] Nozick thinks of each individual's rights as constituting a kind of moral space which others may not enter without permission. Each individual is in principle free to protect his own moral space against incursions by others.

Nozick argues that the only kind of state which could ever evolve from this state of nature and come legitimately to exercise a monopoly of coercive power is a minimal state whose concern is confined to the preservation of security. The reason for treating security as a special case is that it is held to be a benefit for all which all have reason to accept. Such unanimity can come about because as some people combine ever more effectively to defend their own security, the feasibility for others of reliance on individual self-protection diminishes, so that those who might have wished to remain independent are subject to an ever-increasing but legitimate pressure to do otherwise.

The case for the centralized provision of security is in Nozick's view quite different from that for the provision of welfare, since the latter consists of the pursuit of good for some at the expense of others. He is particularly scathing about the appeal to 'social justice' because 'there is no *social entity* with a good that undergoes some sacrifice for its own good. There are only . . . different individual people with their own individual lives.'[21]

So the state which taxes its well-off citizens for redistributive purposes is in effect held to be stealing from them. Nozick does not deny the possibility that some good consequences may result from such taxation. His point is that those who wish to help fellow-citizens poorer than themselves should do so from their own resources, but are not entitled to use the apparatus of the state to deprive others of legitimately acquired wealth. To achieve good results through a redistributive state is thus to commit theft.

But when is wealth legitimately acquired? Transfers of ownership, in Nozick's view, are in normal circumstaces legitimate only if they take place in circumstances which reflect the free choice of the previous legitimate owner. The chief qualification to this generally uncompromising doctrine concerns what he describes as the Lockean proviso. This makes the rights of ownership dependent on there being 'enough, and as good left in common for others'.[22] Although the Lockean proviso is potentially an important qualification, its practical importance for Nozick is diminished by the fact that he interprets it in such a way that he himself thinks it would be unlikely ever to come into effect.[23]

So for Nozick there is in essence no moral requirement that wealth should be distributed equally or in such a way as to ensure that everyone has a certain minimum or according to any other pattern, because the community which is supposed to exhibit this pattern is a fiction. One might for example as readily complain about the fact that some people have lots of friends and others have none. Being friendless may be a great misfortune, but since most of us do not think that the community is responsible for the distribution of friendship, we do not see the fact that some people lack friends as an indication of social injustice.

Nozick's view of the distribution of wealth is undoubtedly bad news for those who do not have the good fortune to inherit wealth and who come on to the scene too late to have much chance of appropriating unowned objects for themselves. What matters though in his opinion is whether there is anything unfair about it. This would only be so, in his view, if resources had been appropriated in a way that infringed the Lockean proviso. From this perspective what matters is not what they can own but what they may use. So if we are fortunate in having a lot of property, this is not unfair to those who have none, so long as our good fortune does not preclude the possibility of a reasonable existence for them. And since a free market system will, he believes, allow all to be materially no worse off than they would otherwise have been, Nozick concludes that a free market system is not unfair to the poor.

Whereas Nozick is at pains to argue for the market society on the ground that it is the product of individuals doing what they have a moral right to do, Hayek's argument has a somewhat different emphasis. He is unsympathetic to attempts to justify *laissez-faire* as a rule to be applied without exception.

> There is nothing in the basic principles of liberalism to make it a stationary creed, there are no hard-and-fast rules fixed once and for all . . . Nothing has done so much harm to the liberal cause as the wooden insistence of some liberals on certain rough rules of thumb, above all the principle of *laissez-faire*.[24]

Hayek's objection here is not to *laissez-faire* as such but to the willingness of some liberals to stand pat on a naked assertion of fundamental rights. This deficiency he seeks to remedy by arguing that economic competition is in general the best means of coordinating human activity. He concedes that there are particular areas, such as the provision of road signs, in which the conditions of competition cannot be created. In the main, however, he claims that competition 'is the only method by which our activities can be adjusted to each other without coercive or arbitrary intervention of authority'.[25] His reason is that good decision-making has to reflect all relevant knowledge. Since modern society is too complex for any planner to have all this knowledge, a planned economy must be inefficient. The only way in which one person's economic activity can be coordinated with that of others is by attending to fluctuations in price. The market enables people to harmonize their activities, because prices provide us in coded form with all the relevant information about other people's activities. But Hayek points out that this will only be true where there is no mechanism that allows producers to control the price, for then they would not need to adapt to meet the demands of consumers.[26] He concedes that there may be particular advantages which accrue from planning,[27] but claims that economic planning always encourages producers to respond to past decisions by bureaucrats and to seek to anticipate and influence future ones. So what is always lost are the unforeseeable advantages that result from the spontaneous actions of free individuals. Moreover we cannot gain any benefits from planning without creating a bureaucratic mechanism which constitutes a framework that can readily be deployed for tyrannical ends, for, he writes, 'whether we should wish that more of the good things of this world should go to some racial elite, the Nordic men, or the members of a party or an aristocracy, the methods which we shall have to employ are same as those which could ensure an equalitarian distribution'.[28] Hayek's theme is thus a development of that of Adam Smith. He holds that in the economic sphere the centralized pursuit of a given objective is counter-productive. If government seeks directly to ensure the efficient production and distribution of goods, it will fail and, worse, it will create the framework which allows some people to tyrannize others.

We are now in a position to observe that there are two kinds of argument that economic liberals may put forward for a free market society. One has its roots in Locke, is echoed by Nozick and emphasizes the sovereignty of the individual and his moral right not to be coerced into doing things against his will even where these things may genuinely be of benefit to others. The other is associated with Smith and Hayek. It is an appeal to the evidence which invites us to conclude that in the economic sphere it is irrational to seek to get individuals to act so as to promote worthwhile community objectives. This is because such attempts involve the destruction of the free market mechanism, which is held to constitute a hidden information base that provides the best system for enabling people to coordinate their activities. So worthwhile social objectives may not be effectively realized by economic planning. And even if they were, this would be at an unacceptable cost.

Of the two kinds of argument, we may observe that Locke and Nozick regard individual rights as having a reality which is prior to actual social arrangements. On the other hand the arguments of Smith and Hayek, although they support broadly similar political rights, seek to underpin these rights in a way that may commend them to those who may have difficulty in regarding rights as a point of departure. It should however be emphasized that the distinction is largely theoretical. Provided the argument for political rights appeals to what are held to be enduring aspects of the human condition, and not just to currently prevailing circumstances, then those who are convinced by it may be as emphatic in their support for these rights as the person who treats them as a point of departure. Before we attend further to this theoretical distinction, let us take some account of another kind of liberalism.

8

Welfare Liberalism

The Limitations of the Market

Rights play a less conspicuous part in welfare liberalism. Nevertheless they remain important. John Rawls, welfare liberalism's most
celebrated contemporary philosopher, combines a commitment to
the equal right of all citizens to basic political and religious freedoms with a supplementary principle designed to limit social and
economic inequalities so that even the worst-off are enabled to
the maximum feasible extent to determine the course of their own
lives. The principle of equal rights is said to take priority over
the principle governing the mediation of social and economic
inequality. So it is clear that rights are at the core of Rawlsian
political life.

These rights however appear to be presented not as a point of
departure but as the product of a particular theory. Although the
precise structure of Rawls's argument has an elusive quality, it is
clear that the principles which embody these rights are justified
as the ones that would be chosen behind a hypothetical veil of
ignorance designed to prevent us simply favouring those proposals
that suit ourselves. We are to envisage ourselves as choosing so
as to maximize our prospects of being able, once the veil is lifted,
to act effectively as rational agents in pursuit of the objectives we
set for ourselves. It has been suggested, though by Ronald Dworkin rather than by Rawls himself,[1] that this argument presupposes
an appeal to a different right, namely each citizen's right to
equal concern in the design of political institutions. Rawls's later
writings seem to make it clear that Dworkin's reading is not

correct, though the fact that the interpretation is possible is an indication that welfare liberalism can proceed from a rights-based starting point. Whether we interpret the Rawlsian principles as being derived from such a right, or whether we view them as embodying the conditions which are most appropriate for rational choosers, it is clear that acceptance of his approach would lead to a community in which the freedom of individuals to determine the course of their own lives would exist within the framework of a constitution designed to give protection not merely against threats such as theft and murder but also against the disadvantages of poverty and social deprivation.

It is appropriate to mention Rawls because he is widely regarded as the leading theorist of welfare liberalism. His influence however has so far been largely confined to academic circles. One reason why he has not been politically influential is the abstractness of his writing. The other reason, to which I have already alluded, is the lack of receptivity in the political climate in that welfare liberalism as a political force has long been in retreat. *A Theory of Justice* was published in 1972, since when there has been no effective government, sympathetic to the ideas of welfare liberalism, anywhere in the Western World. It is appropriate therefore that we should also look to the work of an earlier welfare liberal theorist.

Before doing so however we should note that free market theory, as advanced by Smith and Hayek, holds that the price of goods reflects the degree to which these are desired by the public and the extent to which suppliers are willing to devote themselves to satisfying public demand. The free market is thus cast in the role of an instrument which enables individuals to pursue their own good. It is clear that such a system will only be effective in enabling each person to give proper expression to his own preferences if there is fair dealing within the market. Since an unregulated market would be one within which some would seek to coerce or trick others, the free market cannot be unregulated. Notice that the objection to an unregulated market is not that it would fail to reflect genuine preferences but that it would reflect the wrong preferences. Take the case of a payment made to a blackmailer for the return of an incriminating photograph. Why is it wrong to see this as a legitimate market transaction? Not because such a transaction fails to reflect the preferences of the parties, for the payment will normally reflect the victim's valuation of the importance of avoiding publication. The objection is that the victim's choice is made in unfairly constrained circumstances. The victim genuinely prefers payment to publication, but as a result of the blackmailer's threat is denied the more greatly preferred option of no payment and no publication. A similar consideration applies in the case of monopolies. Most economic liberals are ready to agree that at least some kinds of monopoly are undesirable, but why? The reason is not because monopoly transactions fail to express preferences, but because they are held to express unfairly constrained preferences. So if someone managed to acquire a monopoly of newsprint and used it to ensure that only certain kinds of newspaper were published, the reading public would have a constrained choice. How many copies were sold would genuinely indicate whether people preferred to buy the monopolist's product at the monopolist's price or not to buy a newspaper at all. A desire for a different kind of newspaper would be one that could find no expression within the market place.

The contrast between a free market and an unregulated market serves to underline the fact that the free market should not be seen as something which is spontaneously generated by people acting according to their own desires and which it is the function of politics to protect. Rather the free market is itself the product of political choice and is at best a fair and efficient instrument for allowing people the maximum feasible opportunity to exercise proper control over their own lives. Opposition to blackmail and monopoly indicates that even free market liberals do not think that having proper control over one's life is exactly the same thing as being enabled to implement as many of one's desires as is feasible. Instead their concern is with a sub-set of people's actual desires. This sub-set excludes the desires that people may have when they are subjected to unfair or unreasonable pressures.

Welfare liberals share with economic liberals the desire to maximize the individual's control over his life. What distinguishes them from economic liberals is their view of the range of circumstances which unfairly inhibit this control. Nozick for example holds that market regulation is basically justified only in dealing with those whose interventions leave others worse off. But in his celebrated case for welfare liberalism, Hobhouse pointed out that people may also be prevented from pursuing their individual good by social structures. He wrote that 'a society in which a single honest man of normal capacity is definitely unable to find the means of maintaining himself by useful work is to that extent suffering from malorganization.'[2]

Hobhouse and Individual Self-Determination

In order to grasp Hobhouse's point, we need to see that there is a distinction between those ills for which individuals are culpable in that they have invaded what Nozick regards as the moral space of others and those ills which could be remedied by concerted action but where the remedy is outwith the control of isolated individuals. Hobhouse's point is not simply that life is better for workers if employers are forced to offer them more generous terms, but that the adoption of a free market mechanism itself generates an inappropriate set of desires.

> The majority of employers in a trade we may suppose would be willing to adopt certain precautions for the health or safety of their workers, to lower hours or to raise the rate of wages. They are unable to do so, however, as long as a minority, perhaps as long as a single employer, stand out. He would beat them in competition if they were voluntarily to undertake expenses from which he is free.[3]

So although employers might otherwise be willing to improve working conditions, economic competition may have the effect of subordinating this to their desire to compete successfully. Although no-one may have individual responsibility for the general level of pay or working conditions, Hobhouse's point is that the resultant ills are remediable. In all Western countries there is legislation governing safety in the workplace, and liberally-minded governments like those of Lloyd George and Franklin D. Roosevelt introduced welfare measures designed to ensure that no-one need suffer the direst forms of poverty.

It is plain that this must involve a more interventionist state than that favoured by economic liberals. But these interventions are still characteristically liberal in that they are intended to extend, rather than restrict or mould, the citizen's choice. For the welfare liberal the point of intervention is not simply to give greater material wealth to the poor, but to enable them to become self-reliant. Hobhouse appeals to the 'self-directing power of personality'[4] and holds that the function of the state remains an enabling one in that it is 'to secure the conditions upon which mind and character may develop themselves'.[5] It may intervene in cases where the 'non-conformity of one wrecks the purpose of others'[6] but the overriding concern is that the disadvantaged should *through their own efforts* be able to overcome their difficulties.

> The State may provide for certain objects which it deems good without compelling any one to make use of them. Thus it may maintain hospitals, though any one who can pay for them remains free to employ his own doctors and nurses.[7]

Hobhouse concedes that there is a sense in which such a state exercises compulsion even while permitting citizens not to make use of the services it provides. These services must be funded out of taxation, so that all taxpayers are forced to pay for them. However he does not regard this as a problem because he does not endorse the Lockean right to property. Indeed Hobhouse goes so far as to suggest that each man's rights are subordinate to the common good. But since Hobhouse at the same time insists that society is no more than individuals acting in a coordinated manner,[8] his appeal to the common good does not mark a departure from individualism. Instead he argues for the 'rational self-determination' of individuals.[9] Even when people behave in a way that menaces others they must always be treated as 'rational beings'.

> It is not right to let crime alone or to let error alone, but it is imperative to treat the criminal or the mistaken or the ignorant as beings capable of right and truth, and to lead them on instead of

merely beating them down. The rule of liberty is just the application of rational method.[10]

In other words no sanction, however effective, is justified against those who treat others badly, unless it can be seen as having an educative effect. The aim is that those who behave anti-socially *should themselves decide* to do things differently.

Hobhouse's point of departure is thus not a set of rights, but a particular conception of persons as rational self-determining choosers. In that respect his account resembles the philosophically more complex liberalism of Rawls. In effect he operates with a conception of community in which, with the exception of the insane and 'feeble-minded',[11] each adult is expected to make free rational decisions about his own life. Even in cases where we are dealing with people who have not respected this freedom in others, we are to treat them as rational agents capable of making better judgements in future. As Hobhouse puts it, 'liberty . . . rests not on the claim of A to be let alone by B, but on the duty of B to treat A as a rational being'.[12] This duty however always restricts what B may do to A against his will, so that the political consequence is indistinguishable from the recognition of A's right to be permitted to make his own self-determining choices. It is true that being left to make one's own choices is not the same as being let alone. We have seen that in Hobhouse's view some kind of state intervention may be necessary to ensure that the ability of people to make and implement their choices is not inhibited by social structures. Despite this commitment to interventionism, it remains true that political arrangements are justified by reference to a duty to treat people as self-determining rational choosers. So his position clearly remains an individualist one.

9

Arguing about Liberalism

Despite the apparent differences between economic and welfare liberalism, we have seen that each is strongly committed to individualism. This is characteristically expressed in the emphasis on persons acting and choosing for themselves and on the inclination to allot a central role to a conception of the rights of the individual as limiting the requirements that society can make of him. In the cases of Locke and Nozick, we have seen that these political rights are presented as the expression of underlying moral rights whose existence is independent of any particular political arrangements. The same would be true of Rawls if the Dworkin interpretation were correct. Alternatively perhaps Rawls's position is closer to that of Hobhouse who talks more of duties than of rights, and whose basic commitment is to everyone being able to lead the life of a self-determining rational chooser. Smith, Hayek and Hobhouse, who talk least about rights, all argue that a concern for the good of the community must lead us to respect individual freedoms, be it the freedom to act in our own self-interest or the freedom to direct our lives in the way we choose. All liberal individualists share a commitment to a society which is to be judged by the extent to which individuals may direct the course of their own lives. Whatever rights they need in order best to achieve this are the ones that are at the heart of a liberal society.

Critics of liberalism may enquire where these rights come from. To this question Locke and Nozick in effect reply that the basic rights of liberal society simply are the moral rights that naturally exist prior to the adoption of any particular set of social arrangements. In other words they are viewed as *foundational*,[1] and are thus conceived as a starting-point for political argument. To some people the existence of such rights seems self-evident. But it is clear that propositions asserting foundational rights are frequently contested. If we are ourselves confident in our intuitive liberal convictions, we may deplore the fact that others dispute them. But that they do dispute them is a reason why liberals may wish to find arguments for these rights.

Those who are not liberals will certainly be dissatisfied by attempts to treat these rights as foundational. Especially will this be true of critics who suspect that these allegedly foundational rights are in reality being used to underpin just those practices and policies which are in the liberal's own self-interest. So Locke has been accused of providing no more than an attempted legitimation of the market society of seventeenth-century England[2] and Marxists would accuse Nozick of tailoring a theory to fit a class interest. To impugn the motives of an opponent however is not to show that his views are wrong. To think otherwise would be to ignore the now familiar distinction between explanation and justification. Explanation here is about why a given individual holds a particular position or why that position is widely held within a particular population, whereas justification concerns the rational grounds that support the position. Focusing on explanation has of course a familiar place in polemical dispute. If we understand the motivation that people have for advancing a particular argument, we may have a better idea of where to look in order to find weaknesses in the argument. But as philosophers we should always remember that exposing someone's motivation, however dark or unworthy, is never a substitute for evaluating his argument, because there may well be less than admirable explanations for the dissemination of justified beliefs. We can show this clearly by appealing to a scientific parallel. An early instrument-maker for example might have supported Galileo's view of astronomy because he had a desire to make money selling telescopes. But even if there was someone of whom this was true, indeed even if Galileo himself had been motivated by the prospect of economic gain, it would not show that their professed astronomical beliefs were unjustified.

Rational Justification, Scepticism and Starting Points

Let us step back briefly from the details of the debate on liberalism and consider more generally the relationship between rational argument and the invocation of supposedly foundational truth. Whilst it easy to be suspicious of the assertion of truths which we are supposed to accept as prior to actual evidence or argument, it is equally not possible to dispense with them. Rational justifications have to begin somewhere. Any justification, like for example a mathematical or scientific proof or a logical argument, must begin by taking something for granted. The rational justification of a proposition involves supporting it by advancing other propositions or premises from which it can be derived. But such an attempt to justify a proposition will only be regarded as successful by a hearer who accepts the premises and also accepts the *validity* of the argument, by which is meant that the premises are such that *if true* they demonstrate the truth of the conclusion.

This may be illustrated by taking the example of an argument about discrimination in employment. An employer who is criticized by a liberal for refusing to employ women as building labourers might reply (1) that such jobs should go to those who are physically strongest and (2) that women are on average less strong than men. We can think of these as premises that are cited in favour of the conclusion that women are not to be employed as building labourers.

To find such an argument cogent, we should first of all have to agree with the premises. Either might be disputed, and a doubter might ask the employer to justify them. The problem is that there is a danger that the process of rational argument will lead to an infinite regress. Unless there are some premises that we are ready to take on trust, it is hard to see how there ever could be a cogent argument for anything. Imagine arguing with someone who challenges whether men are on average physically stronger than women. We might try to convince him by conducting a test. Let us, we might propose, take 100 men and 100 women at random and see what weight they are able to lift. The trouble is that the sceptic might challenge us on whether lifting ability is the proper test of strength, on how we know that our random samples really are typical of men and women respectively, and indeed on how we can know that the measurements or observations we make of what our subjects lift are reliable. We may well be able to supply reasons for discounting these doubts, but it does not require much imagination to see that we will simply give the sceptic the possibility of raising a further generation of doubts.

How to respond to sceptical doubts has been one of the enduring themes of modern philosophy. The French philosopher, Rene Descartes, was concerned with the question of how we could ever know anything. His method was to seek to identify some proposition which could not be doubted, and which could then be shown to be the basis of all our knowledge. In his *Meditations*,[3] he argued that it was to be found in the proposition, 'I think therefore I exist', but contemporary philosophers are not ready to agree either that this proposition is beyond doubt or that those other things we think we know about the world can be inferred from it.[4] If we are to conclude with Descartes's critics that the sceptic cannot be refuted, at some point we need either to concede that we know nothing or respond to the question 'How do we know that?' with the answer 'We just do.' And if we encounter some presumptively sane person who apparently doubts whether tables and chairs and buses and trains really exist, we might reasonably dismiss his doubts as not serious. Such a philosophical position, we might suppose, is one that cannot really be *lived* in that the sceptic will not survive unless he seeks to avoid collisions with buses and trains on the assumption that what he professes to doubt might just be true.

The need to take things for granted applies not only in respect of the truth of the premises but also in respect of the validity of arguments. We can imagine someone who accepts the premises of the employer's argument for sex discrimination, but who points out that the conclusion does not follow, because information about the strength of the average woman is irrelevant to a decision about employing a particular woman. The conclusion to the argument after all was not that it is wrong to appoint an averagely strong woman rather than an averagely strong man, but that it is wrong to appoint any woman in preference to any man. In this example most of us will agree that there is something wrong with the logic of the argument. But how do we know this? How can we prove it?

Logic is concerned with the rules of inference that we use in validly deriving conclusions from premises. But the claims of logic are themselves held to be self-evident and not amenable to proof. So from the initial premise

(A)　Bill is the tallest person in the world.

we are just expected to see that we can draw the conclusion

(B)　Every other person in the world is less tall than Bill.

If someone demands that we prove that (B) follows from (A), there is nothing much we can do other than check that he has a normal command of English. We may perhaps say that to accept the initial premise and still allow that someone else may be as tall as or taller than Bill would involve contradicting oneself, but then the determined doubter might ask us for an argument to prove the unacceptability of self-contradiction.

We can never meet such a request to the satisfaction of the doubter, for the simple reason that any supposed proof would be seen as one which itself rests on a similarly questionable assumption, and can therefore be rejected as question-begging. But although we cannot provide a proof that is immune to such an objection, we can make a parallel move to the one that dealt with the sceptic who doubted the existence of trains and buses. Someone who does not see that there is a problem about self-contradiction, we may say, does not have a serious interest in knowing things at all. To know a proposition just is to know that it is true. To know that it is true must involve knowing that it is not false. Those who do not suppose that there is an incompatibility between truth and falsity cannot know any proposition. For if there is no genuine distinction between truth and falsity, there is no incompatibility between any true proposition and its negation. So those who seriously doubted the distinction would also have to doubt the truth of the proposition that there are other people with whom they can engage in argument. If they then persist in demanding of others that they produce some rationale for the undesirability of self-contradiction, we may point out that their engagement in dialogue is itself an indication that their doubts are not entirely serious. If we thought that their doubts were real, we would be concerned for their mental health. If they say that their doubt is not psychological but philosophical, that is they do not really doubt the distinction but are concerned about our inability to provide a rationale for it, we can reply that the sheer *unlivability* of taking the doubt seriously is a powerful indication that no further rationale is needed. But the task of proving the error of scepticism, whether about the existence of material objects or the acceptability of rules of inference, is one that can never be completed. In the end we must be content with the realization that the sceptical position is one that cannot be *lived*. But to say that every argument has to begin somewhere is not to concede that it must be underpinned by a commitment to particular foundational assumptions which we can never have reason to change.

Liberalism and its Foundations

We have reason to suppose therefore that any viewpoint that merits being taken seriously must take something for granted. The person who will never accept any premise as prior to argument can have nothing useful to contribute to the discussion of political or any other ideas. So rights-based liberalism certainly cannot be discredited by the simple fact that it involves an assumption which we are invited to take for granted. But what is striking about Locke and Nozick is the rapidity with which they resort to assumptions which we are to take for granted. For them the political rights which the state must defend are an expression of foundational moral rights for which no argument is supplied.

But there is the possibility of offering some arguments in support of or in opposition to liberal principles. Thus we have seen that Hobhouse views political rights as grounded in the duty to treat others as rational beings who must be allowed to make their own choices. This provides some scope for further debate. How for example does Hobhouse justify his move from this duty to his assertion of a state which is morally entitled to use force to ensure that the duty is carried out? If people do carry out this duty, can we be certain that this will in practice give rise to a society characterized by respect for liberal political rights? In mentioning these questions I do not mean to imply that Hobhouse would have difficulty in supplying satisfactory answers, but to illustrate the point that Hobhouse's arguments have further to run than those of Locke and Nozick. We do not find that we are abruptly invited to accept as self-evident a set of rights which are very similar in nature to the liberal political rights whose justification we seek. In Hobhouse's case the justification stops with the invocation of a particular duty to allow people to act as rational choosers. Even if we think that Hobhouse could supply satisfactory answers to the questions just mentioned, we might still wish to enquire why the life of a rational chooser is to be regarded with more respect than other kinds of life. At this point the chain of justifications comes to an end. Those who wish to assert the existence of a Hobhousian duty might still refer us to the writings of Immanuel Kant or other philosophers, but although we may find liberal assumptions articulated there, it remains true that we are in the end simply invited to make assumptions. These assumptions about foundational moral values, be they rights, duties or conceptions of the good life, may be characterized as *deontological*. Such foundational values are those which are held to be inherently right or to constitute the intuitively obvious features of the world as it ought to be.

We have seen that deontologically-based arguments for liberal practice appeal in some way to the intrinsic desirability of people determining the course of their own lives. In the case of economic liberalism this is interpreted as meaning that people must be no worse off than they would be if others left them alone. Hence rights are in general interpreted negatively, and property rights are endorsed with the qualification that private appropriation must not deprive anyone of the possibility of enjoying a reasonable material standard of living. In the case of welfare liberalism, the assumption is that the community may have to establish a social framework that will enable individuals to determine the course of their own lives.

More will be said in Part Five about foundational values, but we should note that political argument does not terminate with the introduction of a foundational claim. Although it is clear that we cannot go back further in search of something for foundations to rest on in a way that compares with that in which particular political practice may rest on foundations, there are some tests which even foundational claims must satisfy. The first is that foundational values must operate at a high degree of generality. Such values are ones which shape a person's approach to the contingent facts of political life. Because they are foundational, they are not themselves to be defined in a way that directly refers to these facts or to particular political problems. There would be no credibility in claiming foundational status for principles which specify detailed policies. Thus for example one can imagine a person who believes that a foundational value should be love of country. Such a value may be invoked in support of or in opposition to some specific policy proposal. One might however be disinclined to allow someone to appeal to a supposedly foundational value which without further argument specified whether a common currency is desirable for Europe, whether America ought to have funded the Nicaraguan Contras, or whether New Zealand ought to permit ships carrying nuclear weapons to use her ports. So one may always insist that foundational values be spelled out clearly but in terms which are general rather than particular. In turn this may enhance the prospects of raising questions of the kind that I have mentioned in discussing Hobhouse, namely questions about the extent to which the foundational values really do give support to the political doctrines in whose aid they are invoked.

In addition to the requirement that these values should be general, we can also expect them to have some clear and important bearing on what are, or perhaps ought to be, the major concerns of the lives of those for whom the values are advocated. So we would be surprised to encounter in the guise of a foundational political value the assertion of the right of all persons to park their

car in the street outside their house. Those of us who do not
agree that this should be the central concern of people's lives
would reject any attempt to invoke such a right as a foundational
value. If we are to recognize such a parking right at all, we should
need an argument to show that it is rooted in something important,
perhaps freedom of movement. Perceptions of what is important
can of course differ. So it is not logically impossible that someone's
life should revolve around his car-parking opportunities. But
before we could contemplate viewing such a life as desirable, we
should need to believe that it is something more than a mere
theoretical possibility. Here argument would again be relevant.

A third point of debate that may arise once the appeal to a
foundational value is made stems from the fact that such values
on occasion prove burdensome to those who are convinced that
they should live in accordance with them. The attempt to act in
accordance with our principles may give rise to what has been
described as strains of commitment.[5] It is easy enough to see this
if we contemplate religious fundamentalism. Take for example
the objection of Jehovah's Witnesses to blood transfusions. A
Jehovah's Witness who is told that her daughter's life can be saved
only at the cost of a transfusion may find her religious commitment extremely burdensome. Liberalism does not normally face
its supporters with choices quite as stark as that. But the demands
of economic liberalism would prove burdensome for those who
would be discomfited at being confronted with a group of
impoverished fellow-citizens who could be significantly helped
only by state economic aid. Still more might this apply to impoverished liberal parents expected to engender respect for property in
the minds of their children. Or take Hobhouse's claim that criminals must always be punished in a manner that has educational
value so that in future they can make rational choices for themselves in a way that does not menace others. Here he is expressing
his faith in the proposition that each person potentially has the
capacity to make rational choices that determine the course of his
own life in a manner that recognizes the similar rights of others.
But suppose we conclude that this is unlikely to be achieved in
the case of a criminal with a record of repeated serious attacks on
children. One possibility is to impose a penalty that will keep

him out of harm's way at least until he is too old to be a danger. If we follow Hobhouse's recommendation despite our conviction of the improbability of the man mending his ways, may this not give rise to strains of commitment? The significance of such strains will be discussed in Part Five.

Those who reject a deontological approach may be tempted to embrace *consequentialism*. For consequentialists political or moral principles are to be justified by appealing to the consequences of their adoption. The consequentialist must still give an indication of what are regarded as good and bad consequences. In the simplest cases the consequences to be sought are those that are most desired or are thought most conducive to happiness. Such arguments for liberal political rights enable discussion to proceed further, because we can cite evidence about what people desire. Beyond that however we can contemplate the evidence of whether liberal rights really do lead to this outcome. Since different people desire different things and in any case desires may change over time there is a great deal of scope for rational argument. It should be noted however that this does not mean that the need for a prior assumption is avoided. There remains an assumption about the value of satisfying people's desires or of human happiness.

Utilitarianism and Liberalism

In Smith and Hayek there is the hint of consequentialist arguments. The reason for putting the point so cautiously is that my discussion of these writers has shown only that they claim certain pragmatic advantages for liberalism. There is a difference between claiming that a justified practice has certain advantages and claiming that the practice is justified on account of these advantages. Thus a doctor who always tells the truth to her patients may respond to someone who objects that this will cause unhappiness by claiming that her patients are happier because they know they can trust her. If this claim is true it ought to defeat the objection, but this does not commit the doctor to the view that her practice is justified *because* it makes her patients happier. In reality she may think it right to tell the truth not because she believes it will make the patients happier but because she believes that people have a right to know the truth whether or not it makes them happy. Similarly the fact that some liberals claim certain general advantages for their favoured conceptions of liberalism does not indicate that they are liberals on consequentialist grounds. In order to determine whether they are, we would need to engage in a detailed study of these writers that would be outside the scope of this book. But that some have thought that liberalism can be justified in this way is clear beyond doubt, because *utilitarianism*, the philosophy which places just such considerations at the heart of all ethical questions, was first set out in the nineteenth century by two liberally-minded philosophers, Jeremy Bentham and John Stuart Mill.

Utilitarianism in its simplest form maintains that the ultimate criterion of morality is the attainment of the greatest happiness. So those actions are right which produce more happiness, or less unhappiness, than any of the available alternatives. This view is notoriously subject to a number of thorny conceptual problems which, on the assumption they can be resolved, I shall not here explore.[6] Many of its opponents are appalled by its apparent implications for the treatment of individuals.[7] At least at first sight it seems that utilitarians will attach no weight to the fair or just treatment of the individual and will sanction the sacrifice of a small unpopular minority in order to appease the prejudices of a bigoted majority. This way of interpreting utilitarianism was reinforced by Bentham's explicit attack on individual rights, when he wrote that '*natural rights* is simple nonsense: natural and imprescriptible rights, rhetorical nonsense, – nonsense upon stilts.'[8]

Although Bentham was attacking the notion of foundational moral rights rather than the intelligibility of legal rights, it is clear that utilitarianism in such a simple form cannot be a secure foundation for liberal political institutions or practices. It does not matter here whether the rights that the liberal seeks to assert are rights to property and security or other rights supposedly needed if the citizen is to exercise control over the course of his own life. The problem is that although a utilitarian can support legal protection for any given freedom, such support must always be subject to recalculation, much as the hypothetical Polish communist whom we encountered in chapter 7 would always be ready to reconsider his support for freedom of worship.

It may of course be thought a strength of utilitarianism that it should be ready to revise normal moral understandings in abnormal circumstances. Perhaps we should be sympathetic to the flexible view that the rights or freedoms of the individual should never act as a barrier to the pursuit of the general happiness. But whether correct or not it seems to me that what results from such flexibility is not recognizable as liberalism. Consider for example a proposal to intern or expel a group of émigrés on the ground that it is likely or even certain that a small number of them are spies. Whether or not this is something that could reasonably be held to be the correct thing to do, it certainly involves viewing each of these émigrés principally as a member of a particular group rather than as an individual. There can be no pretence that this is a liberal measure. This is not to deny that some liberals might reluctantly support it. But those who take individual rights seriously, even if they thought they had little alternative to the acceptance of such a proposal, would at the very least have to concede that it involves serious injustice.

Despite what seems to be the clearly illiberal nature of utilitarianism, John Stuart Mill claimed that the arguments he advanced for individual freedom in his famous essay *On Liberty* rested ultimately on an appeal to the principle of utility.[9] How could he have thought this? The most likely possibility is that Mill is committed to a more sophisticated version of utilitarianism, called *rule-utilitarianism*.[10] Rule-utilitarianism, by contrast to the simpler version just discussed which we can now call *act-utilitarianism*, holds that in assessing the morality of an action we should appeal not to the likely consequences of that particular action but to the likely consequences of the general rule or practice under which that action can be subsumed. Take the example of the proposal, anathema to liberals, to torture a particular prisoner in order to obtain information that might help apprehend a violent criminal. A supporter of rule-utilitarianism might contemplate not only the likely effects of using torture on this occasion, but also the likely effects of adopting the general practice of using torture on such occasions. These effects might include the risk of a drastic loss of confidence in the police, of liberal police officers resigning and being replaced by sadists, and perhaps even of the destabiliz- ation of the state. The rule-utilitarian may take his estimate of such effects into account, even though he may think of them as highly improbable consequences of a single act of torture, because he views them as possible consequences of adopting the torturing of unforthcoming witnesses as a general practice. This differs from the act-utilitarian who will only take such effects into account if he thinks them likely to result from the one act under consider- ation. It may appear then that the rule-utilitarian is less likely than the act-utilitarian to sanction the resort to a single act of torture, since there is always a good chance of keeping the public from learning about one act, whereas there is no chance of main- taining secrecy about the adoption of a general practice of tortur- ing prisoners. Rule-utilitarianism may therefore look as if it can yield liberal conclusions, because respect for the rights asserted by liberals may seem to be the kind of rule that might be adopted in a rule-utilitarian system.

But is the difference between rule-utilitarianism and act-utili- tarianism more than cosmetic? In order to apply rule-utilitarianism we have to identify the general practice or rule under which a particular action can be subsumed. But this is a function of how we choose to describe the particular action. If we describe the action as 'torturing a prisoner' then making this our general practice is likely to have far-reaching effects. If we describe the action as 'torturing a prisoner in circumstances in which there is minimal risk of publicity', these effects will not apply. The objec- tion is that any act which the act-utilitarian will think it right to perform can be described in such a way as to fall under a rule which the rule-utilitarian would have to adopt. Clearly if the rule- utilitarian adopts the rule, 'Always perform that act which will maximize utility' he will think it right to carry out the same acts as the act-utilitarian. And if the rule-utilitarian really is a utili- tarian, what better rule could he adopt?

Can the criticism that rule-utilitarianism collapses into act- utilitarianism be resisted? The only possibility is by imposing restrictions on what is to count as a rule or practice. Such a restriction may for example have the effect of counting only rules or practices which clearly identify the precise actions that are required and discounting those which are too complicated or too demanding for us to be confident that people would carry them out. Think of a nation fighting a war. Although the attainment of victory is the ultimate objective, soldiers are not instructed to do whatever will be most conducive to victory but to obey the orders of their superior officers. The point here is that the soldiers cannot be expected to identify what will be most conducive to victory, but they can be expected to understand and carry out orders. Similarly instructing people to do whatever maximizes utility will not lead to their doing so. And in terms of feasibility, the instruction 'Do not torture prisoners' can more readily be implemented than the instruction 'Only torture prisoners if the likely benefits in terms of information obtained are very important and there is little risk of publicity.' Once we allow the security forces to engage in torture in the most exceptional circumstances, we run the risk of discovering that they may be easily persuaded that such exceptional circumstances exist.

This gives us reason to suppose that a rule-utilitarian justification for liberal values is possible. Some suitably modified form of the instruction 'Always respect other people's property and personal security' can be counted as the appropriate kind of rule in that we can usually tell which actions fall within its scope. So there is the possibility that the economic liberal can offer a utilitarian justification for giving priority to the rights to security and property. Similarly a welfare liberal might make a case for giving similar status to the right of each individual to self-determination within an economic framework that gives necessary support to the needy.

Yet it is doubtful whether this type of justification can work. Consider first of all the implications for economic liberalism. The empirical claims that we have noted for the free market are that even the poorest may benefit in material terms and that everyone can plan their lives better because they can have more confidence in their expectations about the cooperativeness of fellow-citizens. Of course there could be argument about whether these claims are true. My point is the somewhat different one that even if they are true, this still does not show that free market policies should commend themselves to utilitarians. The reason is that it is far from clear that increased wealth leads to increased happiness.

We do not need to do much empirical research to know that poverty leads to misery, or even that, other things being equal, people prefer more wealth to less. But this does not establish the case made by the utilitarian liberal. The reason is that one person's wealth may well have negative repercussions for the happiness of others. Suppose I am wealthy enough to be able to run a Porsche. Let it be granted that I am happier as a result. But my acquisition of a Porsche may make my poorer neighbours less happy. Why? Because even if they are better off materially than would otherwise have been the case – suppose they cash in by selling me insurance or new tyres for my car – they may feel unsettled by the conspicuous sign of my wealth. And even if one disregards such reactions as prompted by deplorable envy, the pollution produced by my car may make them and their children less healthy, which in turn may make them unhappy.

At first sight this last point sounds like a quibble because the damage to the environment caused by one car is surely minute. Most of us are clear that we prefer having a car to not having one. But of course the negative environmental effects produced by one car, though infinitesimal for one individual, are visited on millions of people. But each individual suffers the negative environmental effects produced by the cars of millions of people. So although, given that whether or not each of us has a car makes no significant difference to the total environmental pollution, we may each be happier with a car than without, we cannot conclude that we would therefore be happier in a society in which there is wide car ownership than in one in which there are no privately owned cars. Indeed if the pursuit of individual wealth has the effect of triggering catastrophic global warming, it will be apparent to all that the pursuit of individual wealth does not lead to the maximization of human happiness.

Quite apart from the possible environmental ill-effects of each individual pursuing his own well-being, there may also be social ill-effects. Even if a free market society is a wealthy society and even if the poor are wealthier than everyone in more egalitarian societies, their relative privation may still be damaging to their self-esteem. Moreover this may communicate itself to their children so that they in turn grow up expecting to fail. The consequence may be the engendering of sullen hostility and social disharmony. This of course is a common socialist criticism of even the most successful Western capitalist states. Such criticism may or may not be thought to be justified. Unless it can be refuted, it will not be enough for a utilitarian liberal to point out that a free market society is a wealthier society.

Perhaps the utilitarian might be attracted to welfare liberalism. Although his argument is not a utilitarian one, we have seen that Hobhouse recognizes that there may be obstacles in the way of people realizing the ideal of self-determination which are more subtle than coercion, theft and fraud. If welfare liberalism would lead to less inequality then it may not be thought to be subject to the same risk of engendering disharmony. But a utilitarian case for welfare liberalism would give rise to its own problems.

The first can be put in the form of a critical question that might well be asked by the economic liberal. Does the welfare state in fact succeed in developing the ability of those who receive benefits to look after themselves, or is the evidence that many of those who obtain benefits simply enter into long-term dependency on the state? Our verdict on this criticism will depend on what we make of the factual evidence.

A second problem mirrors a point made earlier about economic liberalism. Although the welfare liberal recognizes that some people will need help, his ideal is that people should so far as possible shape the course of their own lives. But just as other people's possession of motor cars may have negative repercussions for me, so may the individual decisions of others who seek freely to shape their lives. All of the liberal arguments represent men and women as persons who can and should make rational choices for themselves. Liberal politics and the arguments within liberalism are concerned with extending the range of such choices. But from a utilitarian perspective it is not at all clear that we are best off engaging in the maximum feasible amount of individual decision-making. Constantly making plans for one's future can be a lonely occupation and for some people may be a great burden. So there may be some advantage in participating in collective decision-making. It is true that liberalism does not preclude the possibility of people choosing to do things collectively rather than individually. It does however undermine the attractiveness of such an option because within a liberal society no-one is immune from the social and economic effects of others being free to pursue their own material objectives. So if a group of people, who are not much interested in the pursuit of material wealth, wish to live and work together on a small farm and lead their lives running their joint enterprise together, they are free to do so but they may not be able to acquire the land unless they can raise as much money as the merchant banker who wants it in order to build himself a second home in the country. But in order to achieve this they will have to forsake their ideals in order pursue material wealth. I am not here seeking to suggest that the appeal to utilitarianism will clearly count against liberal individualism or in favour of people living in small collectives. All I suggest is that we have no reason to suppose that the level of general happiness in any community is closely related either to the total amount of wealth generated within it, or to the extent of individual self-determination. At the very least the liberal utilitarian is making great demands of the facts, so that we should need to see a lot of evidence before we are convinced.

Liberalism and Human Nature

We noted earlier that a political ideology offers not only a conception of how a community ought to be governed but also of the good life for the individuals who constitute it. This is because different ideologies involve different conceptions of how individuals relate to the community. We have seen that liberals are strongly committed to the good of rational self-determination. Let us leave aside any doubts that can be raised about whether rational self-determination should be viewed in this light and ask what kind of persons are needed to make a success of such a society?

In terms of moral qualities we can see that liberal citizens should be ready to respect each other. Obviously too little concern for others would be undesirable because it would result in a Hobbesian war as individuals fought for domination. But too great a commitment to others would also be undesirable because it would get in the way of people directing themselves. Liberals do not wish to place any impediment in the way of those who choose to devote themselves to the welfare of the poor or handicapped or sick or elderly, but they will not be enthusiastic for a society which generates a large degree of social pressure on individuals to subordinate their plans for their own lives to looking after others. A liberal society will be one in which people are ready to respect and trust one another but also wary about allowing others to get close to them. The ideal was encapsulated in Rudyard Kipling's poem *If* in which he wrote

> If neither foes nor loving friends can hurt you,
> If all men count with you, but none too much;
> you'll be a Man, my son!

Further Reading

Because of its more overtly ideological nature, much more has been written on economic liberalism than on welfare liberalism. S. Hall's paper, 'Variants of liberalism' in *Politics and Ideology*, ed. J. Donald and S. Hall (Milton Keynes: Open University Press, 1986) draws attention to different forms of liberalism. A. Arblaster, *The Rise and Decline of Western Liberalism* (Oxford: Basil Blackwell, 1984) and D. A. Lloyd Thomas, *In Defence of Liberalism* (Oxford: Basil Blackwell, 1988) offer contrasting approaches. The most useful single volume for approaching this subject is *Liberalism and its Critics*, ed. M. Sandel (Oxford: Basil Blackwell, 1984) which contains extracts from Rawls, Hayek and Nozick as well as contributions from opponents of liberalism. For a discussion of individual and community, see G. Graham, *Contemporary Social Philosophy* (Oxford: Basil Blackwell, 1988). For a philosophical account of the pros and cons of utilitarianism, see J. J. C. Smart and B. Williams, *Utilitarianism* (Cambridge University Press, 1973). For an attempt to apply utilitarian ideas to a particular set of social issues, see J. Glover, *Causing Death and Saving Lives* (Harmondsworth: Penguin Books, 1977). For a view of Bentham's assault on rights, see J. Waldron,

'Nonsense upon stilts? – a reply' in *Nonsense upon Stilts*, ed. J. Waldron (London: Methuen, 1987). For a brief discussion of the philosopher's battle with the sceptic, see B. Russell, *Problems of Philosophy* (Oxford University Press, 1912)

Part III
Conservatism

10

The Conservative Disposition

We are afraid to put men to live and trade each on his own private stock of reason; because we suspect that this stock in each man is small, and that the individuals would do better to avail themselves of the general bank and capital of nations, and of ages. Many of our men of speculation, instead of exploding general prejudices, employ their sagacity to discover the latent wisdom which prevails in them. If they find what they seek, and they seldom fail, they think it more wise to continue the prejudice, with the reason involved, than to cast away the coat of prejudice, and to leave nothing but the naked reason . . .

    Edmund Burke, *Reflections on the Revolution in France*

Different societies have different things to conserve, so we should not expect the detailed character of conservatism to be uniform across the world or remain constant throughout history. When Kremlinologists used to write about conservative opponents of *glasnost* and *perestroika*, they did not mean to suggest any particular ideological affinity between the Party hardliners and latter-day admirers of Edmund Burke. Nor are American conservatives exactly the same as British conservatives. In America the principal opponents of conservatives are welfare liberals, and American conservatism is primarily associated with an emphasis on low taxation. In Britain conservatives have often been challenged by those who wish to bring about institutional change, for example devolution in Scotland and Wales or the abolition of the House of Lords. Nevertheless we can still make worthwhile generalizations because conservatism, at any rate of the traditional kind, is characterized more by a particular kind of approach to politics than by a commitment to particular policies.

Numerous writers in both Britain and America have observed that conservatism involves a disposition or spirit of the human mind.[1] In Oakeshott's words, the general characteristics of this disposition 'centre upon a propensity to use and to enjoy what is available rather than to wish for or to look for something else; to delight in what is present rather than what was or what may be'.[2] Although these writers recognize that such serendipity is neither a sufficient basis for conservatism in a political sense nor confined to those who are politically conservative, it is worth reflecting on the significance of invoking a disposition of character as constituting an important part of the foundations of a system of political belief. The question here is whether the emphasis on disposition indicates a distinctive feature of conservatism. Could we not equally well represent liberalism as the political expression of the disposition to be innovative? We could say that the general characteristics of the liberal disposition centre upon the propensity to seek reasons for what we do not understand and to find newer and better ways of dealing with old problems for ourselves. Similarly, would we not expect to find that socialism or any ideology whatever is likely to be rooted to some extent in authentic dispositions of human nature?

These questions are readily answered. Up to a point we certainly can tell parallel stories for other ideologies. But even if it could be claimed for liberalism that it seeks to tap the capacity for innovation, there is no suggestion that an endorsement of the ideals of liberalism or of liberal policies is itself an innovative act. As for socialism, we shall in due course do what we did with liberalism and consider the characteristics of human beings which are best suited to the kind of society advocated. But socialists do not claim that there is any natural inclination to favour socialist policies which is independent of other arguments that can be advanced for socialism. Indeed in the case of both liberalism and socialism, questions about the connection between the ideology and the motives for which people support it are usually raised by opponents rather than supporters. So critics often claim that classical liberalism is rooted in greed or socialism in envy. Here the objective is to try to discredit opponents by demonstrating that backing for their position stems from something more sinister than they are ready to acknowledge. By contrast what is unusual about the view that conservatism has roots in a disposition of human nature is that the writers who make this point include those who see themselves as ardent conservatives. Although I shall suggest that it is a mistake to see conservatism *principally* as the expression of an emotional disposition, the fact that many conservatives make such claims tells us something important about their view of politics and political argument.

The reason is that our emotional dispositions are not attributes that we choose. Where we recognize that we would be better off without a particular disposition, for example jealousy or timidity, we cannot bring this about simply by resolving that we should change. But we do have a certain capacity for self-control so that once we recognize our failings, we may endeavour on particular occasions to behave in a way that belies these dispositions. So a soldier in battle may not readily be able to dispel his fear, but he can try to appear unafraid. In this he may succeed whilst still being frightened. What this suggests is that emotions or instincts should not be seen as right or wrong in the same way as actions. Thus a man whose natural disposition is to be sexually attracted to small children can readily be criticized for acting in accordance with this disposition, but not so readily for possessing the disposition itself. His predilection may represent a moral imperfection, but a realistic critic will demand only that he controls himself, not that he perfects his character. Our dispositions of character, particularly as we get older, are to be seen as fairly well fixed, but, although we may be subject to great strains of commitment, we may still be able to decide when to act in accordance with them and when to exercise restraint. Dispositions, including the conservative disposition itself, are not states to which those who lack them can readily be converted.

So the emphasis which many conservative writers place on disposition is an indication that their objectives are limited and that they do not see politics as an arena in which to conduct a search for fundamental truth. Conservatives, according to Quintin

Hogg, seek to 'criticize and mould the latest heresy of the moment'[3] but themselves claim no monopoly of truth. This may seem a logical position for such a conservative to take. A society consisting exclusively of conservatively disposed citizens would be without innovators. Hogg's claim that conservatives accept that 'the public good is attained by the interplay of rival forces, of which they recognize themselves to be but one'[4] may be seen as an acknowledgement of this point. However, although dispositions cannot readily be seen as right or wrong, they can be seen as welcome or unwelcome. Selfishness for example is not something of which conservatives approve, and of course they think that it is the function of government to combat particular forms of behaviour which are motivated by selfishness. But that is different from supposing that it is possible to eradicate selfishness. But conservatives are normally ready to recognize that 'there are inherent limitations on what may be achieved by political means (and) man is an imperfect creature with a streak of evil as well as good in his inmost nature'.[5]

However although human dispositions cannot be changed abruptly, some of them are susceptible to gradual change as a result of exposure to the influence of family, friends, colleagues and other associates. Obviously it is younger people who are most amenable to such influence and so conservatives place great emphasis on school and family as sources of moral education. Organized religion also has a key role to play in underpinning social morality. In Burke's words, 'we know, and what is better we feel inwardly, that religion is the basis of civil society, and the source of all good and of all comfort'.[6] This view has persisted even amongst twentieth-century conservative writers. Hogg for example went so far as to claim that 'there can be no genuine Conservatism which is not founded upon a religious view of the basis of civil obligation'.[7]

What is interesting here is Burke's emphasis on inner feeling rather than rational conviction and the persistence of the emphasis on religion as the source of moral standards. The idea that social morality requires a religious foundation is certainly problematic. The nature of the difficulty was first expounded by Socrates. The argument, advanced in *The Euthyphro*, is that one cannot simultaneously maintain that the gods are the source of morality and respect them for their ability to discriminate good and evil. The contention is that if we locate the source of morality in divine authority, then to say that something is morally good is simply to say that the gods approve of it. But do the gods only approve of good things, or do they sometimes approve of what is evil? The argument against seeing morality as determined by divine authority is that this question becomes a trivial one. Naturally the gods only approve of those things of which they approve, but this is equally true of everyone else, whether the moral judgements they make are admirable or contemptible. Why should *we* approve of the things of which the gods approve, unless we think that the things of which they approve are worthy of approval? But if the objects of which the gods approve are worthy of approval, then this worthiness cannot consist in the fact that the gods approve of them. This argument is in principle unaffected if for the gods of ancient Athens we substitute the God of Judeo-Christian morality.

So it might be argued that the appeal to religion is not a philosophically secure basis for civil religion. The above argument may not win universal assent. But perhaps whether the argument should be accepted as cogent matters less than we might imagine. The point is that many people do still believe that religion is a source of moral authority. What our quotations from Burke and Hogg indicate above all is not their commitment to religion, but to something subtly different, namely the social value of people being religious.

Authority, Tradition and the Nation

Respect for authority is a general feature of conservative attitudes. It underlies the emphasis on tradition. Why does the Queen ride through London in a stage-coach on her way to open each session of Parliament? The answer is tradition; her doing so is a symbol of the time-hallowed authority of the Crown. Such answers appeal to respect for the past and to the merits of a constitutional system of which the ceremonial opening of Parliament is but a part. A

British conservative may concede that there could be reasons, for example based on a terrorist threat to the Queen's personal safety, for discontinuing the practice. The point of his approach however is to suggest that it is a mistake to isolate some particular aspect of constitutional practice and demand to know the reason for it. In the absence of obvious objection to a given instance of constitutional practice, it is sufficient to realize that it is one part of a system that has endured for generations. One contemporary conservative theorist describes the approach in the following terms.

> A conservative is 'for' certain things: he is for them, not because he has arguments in their favour, but because he knows them, lives with them, and finds his identity threatened (often he knows not how) by the attempt to interfere with their operation. His characteristic and most dangerous opponent is not the radical, who stands squarely against him, armed with myths and prejudices that match his own, but rather the reformer, who always acting in a spirit of improvement, finds reason to change whatever he cannot find better reason to retain.[8]

This idea of continuity, which holds that a given community has an enduring identity which survives its individual members, is an indication that conservatives tend to adopt an organic rather than an individualist view of community. Conservatism, in Scruton's words, 'presupposes the existence of a social organism. Its politics is concerned with sustaining the life of that organism, through sickness and health, change and decay.'[9] The organic view emphasizes historical continuity and the belief that a political community is more than the totality of the individuals who constitute it at any given time. In terms of the distinction we drew in chapter 7 we may think of traditional conservatives as communitarian rather than individualist. An organism is an entity whose individual parts cannot be said to have any interests of their own, which are independent of the interests of the whole organism. So although our white corpuscles may perish in large numbers as they resist an infection that threatens our health, we do not describe this as a sacrifice. Similarly, if I raise my hand to prevent a stone hitting me in the face, I will not be inclined to say that I put the interest of my face before that of my hand.

We should not ascribe to conservatives the view that there are *no* individual interests distinct from those of the community, because talk of the community as a social organism is ultimately a metaphor. But its use indicates an approach which is quite different from that of the liberal who sees politics as properly concerned with enabling individuals to pursue their own chosen objectives. Conservatives not only honour the traditions of the past, but also recognize duties to the community and to its future welfare. The welfare of a community, understood in this way, means not merely the happiness of its individual members, but the recognition that the good of these individuals is bound up with the community. By this I mean to impute to conservatives the view that not merely will individuals fail to achieve their own good without an appropriate social framework, but that the objectives of individuals should reflect an involvement in the community. A good analogy is to be found in the different attitudes that people have to the role of parent. One kind of parent (the 'liberal') may take the view that the most important objective should be to seek to bring up one's children so that they are well equipped to succeed in the pursuit of their chosen aspirations, always assuming that they respect the rights of others to lead their lives in their own way. If the children are fair in their treatment of others and derive satisfaction from their lives, then 'liberal' parents will feel themselves to have been successful, even if the children emigrate and their contented lives include little subsequent social interaction or even communication with other members of the family. More 'conservative' parents might regard this as something of a failure and attach importance to their children feeling a bond with other members of the family.

In talking of the family I have put the terms *liberal* and *conservative* in quotation marks, because there is no contradiction in being conservative in one's view of the family and liberal in one's view of the community. But the 'conservative' view enables us to understand the kind of significance that conservatives attach to the idea of a *nation*. Those who see a nation as an organism emphasize the importance of patriotism. Just as members of a close-knit family are not simply people who wish each other well but people whose aspirations are influenced by their concern for each other, patriots are not merely people who wish good things for their country but people whose aspirations and satisfactions are in part determined by the fact that they identify with their nation. They may express their commitment by displaying enthusiasm for the symbols of the nation, such as the flag, or they may sing the National Anthem with fervour and show deference to the person and office of Head of State. Their lives are enhanced by national successes. These successes may be won in battle or in the symbolic conflict of international sport, or in economic or scientific endeavour. Conversely national failures or defeats may be seen as a kind of humiliation. Patriots may even feel threatened or affronted by fellow-citizens who do not share their enthusiasm. Most obviously this occurs in the context of the most extreme of patriotic endeavours, namely war. Consider for example the obloquy heaped on American opponents of the Vietnam War who burned their draft cards, and on those in Britain who held that the Falklands War was not a simple victory of right over wrong.[10] I do not mean to suggest either that patriotism always gives rise to intolerance or that only conservatives can be patriots. But emphasis on patriotism as a prime virtue complements the other aspects of conservatism that we have noted in that patriotism, being a kind of love, is a matter of instinct and emotion rather than rational judgement.

The commitment to an organic view of nationhood underpins other aspects of conservative political doctrine. Take for example the well-known stress on law and order. At first sight this may not sound very different from the economic liberal's emphasis on security of the person and the protection of property. But this would be to overlook the importance of the demand for *order*. Liberals are concerned with the fair treatment of individuals, but the traditional conservative is at least as concerned by the need to reinforce the cohesiveness of the nation. No organism can thrive unless its individual parts act harmoniously. If they fail to do so the damage is widespread and unpredictable. The effective functioning of the apparatus of government is thus an essential feature in the life of any nation and the conservative demand for law and order is one aspect of the desire for social harmony which is reinforced by an emphasis on discipline in such matters as the treatment of young offenders, as well as in the home and in schools. Likewise conservatives place a high priority on moral education. According to Mr William Whitelaw, who became Deputy Prime Minister and the leading representative of traditional conservatism in Mrs Thatcher's administration, 'the government must show that it will stand against those who are seeking to undermine the moral standards upon which the vast majority of our people believe our society and family life depend'.[11]

The commitment to a socially cohesive community also helps explain the traditional conservative approach to the needy which is captured in the motto *'noblesse oblige'*. In other words those who have the good fortune to occupy privileged positions have a duty to ensure that provision is made for those less privileged. If they fail to do so they make their own privileges vulnerable since 'a populace never rebels from passion for attack, but from impatience of suffering'.[12] So traditional conservatives have different reasons from welfare liberals for being committed to the idea of a welfare state. But their support is as strong. As Winston Churchill put it in describing the provision needed for those unable to stand on their own feet, 'we shall have a good net and the finest social ambulance service in the world'.[13]

The organic view of community also helps explain another characteristic conservative outlook, namely the attitude to change. The well-being of an organism, it seems reasonable to suppose, does not normally involve abrupt changes of direction or the sudden pursuit of new objectives. An animal does not change its diet where its traditional food is available in sufficient quantity. It would be a mistake however to suppose that conservatives view all change as bad. On the contrary if an organism is to thrive it must be able to adapt to new circumstances, since, to quote Burke once more, 'a state without the means of some change is without the means of its conservation'.[14]

Burkean conservatives can then readily embrace the change that comes as a measured response to the pressure of events in a changing world. They must be ready to bow to what Harold Macmillan once described as the 'winds of change'.[15] What they abhor are avoidable large-scale changes which are embarked on in pursuit of theoretical ideals such as liberty or social justice or as social experiments. The political approach of conservatism is rooted in practice not theory, and involves the prevention, and where necessary resolution, of conflicts that threaten the peace. Arguing along such lines, Oakeshott talks about government as the avoidance of 'collisions'[16] and this suggests a helpful way of viewing conservatism. If we think of the political enterprise as a voyage, liberals and socialists may be viewed as people who wish to set sail for distant destinations. We may also discern some genuine reactionaries, French monarchists perhaps, who wish to return to a port from which the ship has long departed, or some do-nothings who wish to stand at anchor wherever they happen to be. The concern of the conservative in this nautical parable is to give short shrift to all these navigational suggestions. His anxiety is that commitment to any of them may lead to shipwreck, and his preference is to concentrate on keeping the ship afloat. This task does not require masterly inactivity. It involves steering the ship to avoid storms and rocks and dangerous currents, and maintaining both the fabric of the vessel and the morale of the crew.

We are now in a position to identify a distinctly conservative view of what constitutes the good life for an individual. In so doing we must not lose sight of the point made earlier, namely that the organic view of society, if it is to be taken seriously, must ultimately be regarded as a metaphor. As we saw, in a real organism, it does not make sense to suppose that any individual parts have interests of their own. But individual human beings, however committed they are to the well-being of the community to which they belong, patently always do have independent purposes and interests of their own. The good life for an individual citizen, as conservatives conceive it, is to fulfil his or her role in an ordered community and to uphold the settled values of that community. As Burke put it, in describing the prize that France had lost, what is to be sought is 'a protected, satisfied, laborious and obedient people, taught to seek and to recognize the happiness that is to be found by virtue in all conditions'.[17]

11

Arguing about Conservatism

In talking about how conservatism can be subject to rational scrutiny, I shall start by considering the conservative attitude to change. As with liberalism, our immediate objective is not to try to show that conservatism is untenable, but to draw attention to difficulties which a convincing defence of conservatism must surmount. A common criticism is that conservatism is geared to the interests of those who have the good fortune to be well-placed in the community and has little to say to those who are disadvantaged. The Burkean injunction, which in effect is to work hard and be happy, may be viewed as one whose greatest appeal will be to those who have the greatest cause for satisfaction with their present position. It is certainly true that most of the conservative arguments we have considered are *reactive* in that they contemplate how abrupt and large-scale change is to be resisted, how conflicts and collisions are to be avoided and how heresies are to be moulded. In Scruton's words the conservative is 'concerned solely with the task of government'.[1] So even if conservatives sometimes think it right to respond positively to demands for change, it looks as if they are never in the business of initiating them.

But this might be thought to ignore an important aspect of politics. In chapter 3 we defined politics in terms of human activity undertaken in pursuance of beliefs about how the affairs of a community ought to be regulated. This definition incorporates action taken by citizens who may not have a complete set of opinions about how the country should be governed, but who have convictions which relate to particular issues. Those who devote all their political energies to campaigning for abortion on demand, or for the renunciation of nuclear weapons, have objectives that fall short of seeking to govern the country. When is it reasonable for a citizen to campaign for a particular policy? Because conservatism as so far described is reactive, it may be thought to have nothing to say to those who contemplate whether it is right to campaign for particular changes, other than to take the Burkean course and encourage everyone to be satisfied.

Is conservatism entirely managerial in its approach to politics? Is conservative political theory addressed only to some people and is its content solely concerned with how they are to control others? To answer these questions we need to consider the conservative attitude to the place of reason in political argument. So far we have portrayed conservatism as entailing a somewhat sceptical approach to politics. Compared with liberals, conservative theorists have a relaxed view of the need to articulate foundational values. Often they appear doubtful of the wisdom of constantly demanding reasons or justifications for practices that have stood the test of time. Instead we have seen that conservatives appeal to authority and instinct and the preservation of tradition. Some readers may wonder whether this can be reconciled with my earlier claim that politics is an area of discourse which is characterized by rational argument. Indeed the chief enterprise of this entire book, which is to indicate the relevance of philosophy to politics, is viable only if politics is taken to be a subject about which those of differing views enter into rational debate. So if conservatism is a totally non-rational approach to the affairs of a community, then either it should be viewed as a non-political phenomenon or the whole of this book can be consigned to oblivion. In fact although it is right to draw attention to the conservative emphasis on authority and instinct, there is another important part of the story.

One of the impressions that colleagues in other disciplines have of professional philosophers is that they are whimsical men and women with an apparent love of paradoxes. At the risk of reinforcing this slightly disrespectful view, one might observe that in fact philosophers are not so much apparent lovers of paradoxes, but lovers of apparent paradoxes. What philosophers enjoy about the appearance of paradox is the challenge and the opportunity to show how it can be dispelled. There is certainly an air of paradox about the conservative view of rationality; I shall attempt to dispel it, and in so doing indicate what I take to be a critical point in the conservative approach.

Let us first note that an emphasis on instinct and emotion is not incompatible with an appeal to rational argument. Emotions are not susceptible to rational assessment in that, as we have seen, it makes little sense to question whether human beings *ought* to be subject to emotional experiences such as pride, anger, nostalgia, grief, love, hate or fear. It simply is a fact of nature that we are. But emotions are also typically belief-dependent in that we frequently seek to justify them by pointing to certain facts in the light of which particular emotions are held to be appropriate. So factual beliefs will usually be cited in response to such questions as 'Why are you angry with her?' or 'Why do you hate immigrants?' or 'What makes you proud of Jack Nicklaus?' The factual beliefs that figure in honest answers to such questions will on occasion be unsupported by the evidence or even demonstrably false. We may not always succeed in persuading the person who gives such an answer that his belief is wrong, but if confronting him with the evidence makes no difference, we may be inclined to conclude that the emotion is irrational. Also some answers, even if true, seem inappropriate to the emotion. Thus to take the question about Jack Nicklaus as an example, we expect some answer such as 'I taught him how to swing a golf club.' If instead we get the answer, 'My aunt once shared a taxi with his grandmother', we conclude either that the person who gives it is confused in thinking that what he is experiencing is pride or that such pride is irrational. This latter possibility would not of course mean that it lacked a psychological cause. Irrational emotions are not random manifestations. I may be angry with my wife or children after someone has behaved badly to me at work, but this is irrational in that my anger is misplaced. A woman may hate all black people because she was mugged by one black person. So emotions may be real but irrational. Thus, although we cannot raise general questions about the rationality of emotion, we can sensibly raise questions about whether particular instances of emotion are irrational.

So there is no need to deny that patriots may engage in rational judgement. There is certainly scope for reasoned debate about how to express patriotism. The German officers who sought to assassinate Hitler in 1944 made a judgement that he had betrayed the honour of the Fatherland. Their view was that those who supported him for supposedly patriotic reasons were either confused in supposing themselves to be patriots or guilty of misplaced patriotism. But readiness to engage in reasoned debate about the appropriate way for a patriot to act or about whether patriotism is sometimes misplaced does not mean that love of country is seen as something that itself either needs to be or can be rationally justified. There is simply no scope for rational argument about whether to be patriotic in the first place. But we need not find this problematic since we have already seen that rational arguments can only start once some assumptions are taken for granted. There is no reason why the value of patriotism cannot figure as such an assumption.

As for the Burkean suggestion that we are wrong to be constantly seeking reasons, such scepticism about rationality does not entail that we ought to do or believe things for which there is no reason, but simply that we ought to be ready to do or believe things for which *we* are unable to provide a justification. This may sound puzzling, but as noted in chapter 6 we frequently have reasons for believing propositions, even though we cannot give a reasoned justification for the propositions themselves. An alternative way of making the point would be to draw a distinction between different kinds of reasoned justification. This distinction would not be the same as the one made in chapter 2 between explanatory and justifying reasons, but a distinction between justifying a proposition *simpliciter* and justifying belief in a proposition. To go back to an earlier example, even if I, a non-scientist, am unable to cite any evidence that justifies the proposition that light travels at 186,000 miles per second, I may still have a good reason for believing it, namely that those whom I know to be competent physicists have told me that it is true. In this case, although I cannot justify my belief *simpliciter*, I have reason for being confident that others can. So in the second sense I can justify my belief in the proposition.

The conservative contention is that we have good reason to be sceptical of our ability to offer justifications, in the first sense, for supporting particular policies. But this limited scepticism does not preclude the possibility of justifying such policies in the second sense. Moreover the conservative contention itself is one which can be justified in the first sense. This accords well with the quotation with which our discussion of conservatism began. What Burke does is to laud prejudice over reason not because of any antagonism to reason but because he sees prejudice *as containing reason hidden within it*. So the conservative approach does claim the merit of being rationally justified; it purports to state rational grounds, based on the fallibility of individuals, not for abandoning but for limiting the appeal to reason.

We can understand how there can be a rational case for taking such a view of the appeal to reason by reflecting on Oakeshott's account of a man whose hobby is fishing.[2] If his entire purpose is to catch fish, it is obviously important for him to have the most efficient equipment. But if he wishes to enjoy a few hours' peaceful activity exercising his skill, then he can make do perfectly happily with equipment which gives him at least some chance of making a catch. This is what we all know to be the prevailing attitude of amateur fishermen. They do not see the choice of equipment and clothing in purely functional terms, and indeed are quite likely to be attached to clothes that are almost worn out and rods that have been in use for decades. In general the time and money they spend trying to catch fish are not seen as investments to be set against the value of the catch. They go out with the intention of enjoying fishing. Such people do have an objective in mind, in that they really are trying to catch fish, but they are not single-minded about it. They also wish to have the enjoyment which comes from exercising their skills in a pleasant environment. Thus their time is not necessarily wasted if they fail to catch any fish and their enjoyment would not be enhanced by providing them with ultra-efficient equipment which would enable even unskilled beginners to be successful.

A similar point may be made about social activity. Some personal associations are predominantly for the realization of a particular purpose. Professional relationships are often like this, but even here one should note that associating with people professionally may well lead to the dilution of single-mindedness and the development of more personal bonds. Other relationships, such as those between friends,[3] or members of the same family, have a value which is wholly independent of the realization of any particular objective. Having friends or identifying with the other members of one's family may be seen – like the pursuit of a hobby such as fishing – as part of what makes life worthwhile; such relationships constitute the framework of existence. When something is part of such a framework, it does not need to be justified by reference to some external purpose. We know not to expect any answer more enlightening than the hackneyed 'Because they're there' if we ask a mountaineer why he climbs mountains. Similarly we know that people do not normally undertake a cost-benefit analysis of parenthood before they decide to have children. Scruton argues that the state simply is the political expression of the fellowship of a community, so that although it does pursue particular purposes, this is not the most important thing about it.

> It is the mark of rational intercourse that aims are not all predetermined, that some ends – perhaps the most important ends – remain to be discovered rather than imposed. And in the life of society they are discovered not by the perusal of utopian treatises, but, primarily, through participation. And that means sharing in the arrangements wherein the ends of political conduct have their life.[4]

So the conservative view is that desirable political objectives are not items to be proposed by academic experts or insightful political theorists. We cannot successfully prescribe objectives without a good grasp of present reality. According to Scruton what is needed is a statesman 'whose identity bears the impress of the state and who seems to act and speak for interests that are simultaneously the state's and his own'.[5] Many conservatives would however see danger in Scruton's emphasis on the leadership role of a particular individual. Burke is a more typical figure and his view was that political power was best exercised by those with deep roots in the community.

Here, as in our discussion of rule-utilitarianism, we may make use of the analogy of an army fighting for national survival. Admittedly war, unlike politics, is a context in which there is a clear objective. Nevertheless the analogy is relevant because what goes on in a community and in the course of military conflict are both endeavours in which it is vital that activities be successfully coordinated. One might suppose that it is better for a commanding officer to have had a great deal of practical experience in the field than to have spent all his time as a student of strategy. Partly this is because he will then have a better idea of the capacity of his army, but also because the army itself may be readier to carry out his orders if it feels the commander to be 'one of us' rather than an armchair strategist. Similarly it can be held that the wisest forms of government and the best policies do not result from painstaking debate about the requirements of the future but are simply the product of the practical experience of the past.

Undoubtedly there is something to be said for this reasoned attack on excessive reliance on reason. Even if human beings adopted forms of government purely at random, we would still be able to construct an evolutionary argument for supposing that the mere fact that a particular practice had stood the test of time would be an indication that it had merits which may not have been apparent to its initiators and may have escaped its critics. How might such a case be argued?

The Evolutionary Argument

Consider the case of biological adaptation. A genetic mutation that confers no advantage on affected animals or plants will not be widely disseminated. So the fact that a particular gene has become widely disseminated is a reason for supposing that it has conferred some advantage on the individuals which bear it, even if we do not know what that advantage is. Similarly it may be argued that the least appropriate forms and practices of government would have been abandoned because communities which practised them would not thrive. So what remains is likely to have advantages even if no-one can articulate them. We need then to look to history.

The appeal to history shows that the organization of the affairs of any community is so complex that no-one who wishes to bring about radical change can be confident that an attempt to realize his desired objectives will succeed or that it will not also have unanticipated consequences. This latter possibility will not matter to the radical who is sufficiently single-minded, in the same way that the use of dynamite to blow up the salmon in a river will not matter to a fisherman who is single-minded in his desire to catch fish. But just as most fishermen are not in this sense single-minded, so those who loathe a given regime may also have other objectives and concerns beyond its destruction. The lesson of history is that disruption and death on an enormous scale have occurred in the wake of liberal revolutions, like the French Revolution, and socialist ones, like that in Russia. In circumstances in which normal landmarks are abandoned, human beings have shown abundant evidence of their ability to do the most appalling things to each other. Those who are not single-minded have reason to be distrustful of the clear-sighted pursuit of simple objectives.

Does the evolutionary argument give us good reason to suppose that there are likely to be hidden merits in arrangements that have endured for generations? The appeal to evolution works very well when we are contemplating how animals or plants have developed properties that are advantageous to them. Giraffes did not acquire long necks because their ancestors hankered to reach the leaves of the acacia trees. In the animal kingdom changes result from genetic mutations and these really do occur at random; there is no propensity for a mutation to be useful, as opposed to neutral or disadvantageous, but those that are not useful do not endure because they give the animal no advantage over its competitors which would enable it to be more successful in rearing offspring. What we need to remember however is that evolutionary biology does not teach us that any species becomes well adapted to its existence. It teaches that it either adapts or dies.

Our concern however is not with the biological attributes of human beings, but with their social practices. Here it is clear that changes do not occur at random. A social practice does not die only when it leads to the death of the practitioners, but also – and much more commonly – when people become convinced that it needs to be abandoned. Absolutist monarchies for example have tended to fall by the wayside not because the societies which they governed ceased to exist, but because absolute monarchs ceased to command the support they needed. The reason for the loss of support is to be found in the perceptions of those on whom absolute monarchs relied. But such perceptions are shaped and reinforced by, amongst other things, the reasoned protests to which the practice of absolute monarchy gave rise. Moreover, once people are convinced of the need for change, they do not substitute just any alternative, but something which they expect to be an improvement. So for example the French Revolution did not simply result in the overthrow of the Bourbons but also in a commitment, at any rate in principle, to the ideal of equal citizenship.

Whether or not revolutions tend to have much success in attaining the ideals with which they start out, the fact that political arrangements are frequently judged by the effectiveness with which particular objectives are attained offers us some reason to expect that disastrous practices may well be abandoned before they bring about the destruction of the communities affected by them. So we may conclude that the fact that a practice has endured over generations and has not been abandoned is some indication that it may have advantages which are not immediately apparent. But the argument presupposes that people have been ready to complain loudly about the disadvantages. Take slavery. For many years slaves had no way of complaining that would effectively command the attention of those, or even the associates of those, who enslaved them. At the beginning of the nineteenth century the evolutionary argument might have led us to suppose that the fact that slavery had endured for a long time was a reason for believing that it must have advantages. Such an observation would not have been wrong, but at this historical distance we can be confident that the advantages were overwhelmingly for people other than the slaves. That slavery was abolished was at least in part because people who were not of conservative disposition

made a previously indifferent public conscious of the oppress-
iveness of the practice.

Another example can be found in the introduction of laws to
combat dangerous and unhealthy working conditions in factories.
In Britain some of the most important legislation was introduced
by the Conservative government of Benjamin Disraeli. This
accords well with a conservative readiness to respond to widespread and strongly felt grievances. But it is hard to believe that
this would have happened without the attention focused on the
issue by socialists and others. So the extent to which the endurance
of a practice is an indication of its merit is itself a reflection of
people's readiness to campaign to bring about what they view as
improvements. The readier people are to respond to calls for
change, the more confidently we can view the endurance of a
practice or institution as an indication of merit. Conversely the
greater the number who are conservatively disposed, the weaker
the ground for supposing that the mere survival of the institution
or practice is an indication of merit.

It appears then that the force of the evolutionary conservative
argument for having confidence in our traditions and instincts
depends upon the fact that these have been shaped in part by the
activities of those who were not ready to be satisfied with existing
arrangements. Even if we accept the conservative contention that
we have good reason not to disregard the legacy of history in the
constant pursuit of improvement, we also have reason to value
that pursuit. If history had been shaped entirely by those who
were ready to accept change only in response to perceived social
pressure, there would have been no history.

The conclusion that should be drawn from the evolutionary
argument is thus that the quest for political improvement should
be informed by a cautious awareness that practices and institutions
which have survived for a long time may have advantages that are
not immediately apparent. But this presupposes that there is also
some merit in the reasoned pursuit of innovation and reform.
Evidence that long-standing social practices have in the past had
advantages that were not immediately apparent can be seen as a
reason for looking harder than we might otherwise have done at
the arguments for particular changes. It certainly does not by

itself furnish us with a conclusive reason for always allying ourselves with those who cast themselves as the custodians of continuity and tradition against those who demand innovation and
reform.

Is Conservatism Purely Reactive?

This kind of consideration accords with Hogg's point that conservatives see themselves as but one political force and claim no
monopoly of wisdom. This point presupposes not merely the
existence of other more radical political forces but also their value,
for without the radicals there will be no heresies to mould or
demands to temper. But if radicals and conservatives both have
valuable contributions to make, what reason is there for being
conservative? Yet the very title of Hogg's book, *The Case for
Conservatism*, indicates that he does believe that the conservative
approach contains more wisdom than that of their opponents.
So Hogg is recommending that his readers adopt a conservative
approach on the assumption that *others* will not do the same.

The appeal to what would happen if everyone did the same was
encountered in our discussion of utilitarianism. In order to make
such an appeal we have first of all to determine the appropriate
action-description. For example suppose that we are worried
about the well-being of an elderly neighbour whom we have not
seen for days and decide to do something which amongst other
possibilities can be described as 'entering her house without permission' or 'checking that she is safe'. It is clear from this case
that our view of the prospect of everyone doing the same is likely
to depend on which action-description we opt for. Of course, as
in this example, some possible action-descriptions will be more
appropriate than others. Usually we may think that the appropriate characterization is one that best captures the intentions of the
person performing the action. But clearly this cannot always be
a conclusive consideration, for psychopathic murderers may think
of their actions as 'carrying out God's will' and terrorist killers
may see what they do as 'eradicating injustice'.

Usually people ask what would happen if everyone did the

same in order to criticize someone else's behaviour, but we need to reflect on the circumstances in which the fact that it might be self-defeating or bad or absurd if everyone did the same should be seen as a criticism. Suppose someone says that one ought always to sit next to one of the emergency exits on an airliner. A hearer might say, 'But what if everyone did the same?'. In such a case it is clear that not everyone can sit next to an emergency exit, because no passenger aircraft can be economically designed in a way that will allow all the passengers to do this. If however the speaker had simply been giving advice to a friend rather than seeking to propose a policy for reducing casualties amongst passengers, it would not have been relevant to draw attention to the fact that not everyone can sit next to an emergency exit.

Take a concrete example from British politics. Mr Norman Tebbit, when he was Employment Secretary, was interpreted by his opponents as having advised unemployed people to 'get on their bikes' and leave home in order to find work.[6] If we view Mr Tebbit as addressing a certain section of the population, namely those who are enterprising, mobile and who command sufficient resources to find housing in another part of the country, then he could be seen as offering sensible advice. As a general policy prescription, however, it is appropriate to point out that it suffers from the defect that not everyone can achieve it and indeed if all the jobless did leave the areas of high unemployment, their employment prospects might not be greatly enhanced.

Giving practical advice to individuals about where to sit in an aircraft or how to find work can be seen as simply addressing a limited audience. The fact that the usefulness of the advice would be undermined if everyone acted on it does not matter, because the point is that it is not addressed to everyone. The person giving advice to a friend worried about flying is addressing only that friend, not proposing a policy for increasing the safety of air transport. Mr Tebbit's remark is uncontroversial if it seen as similarly addressed to a limited audience. A purely reactive conservatism is concerned only with giving practical advice on how *we* should respond to the demands for change that are initiated by *others*. However political issues arise not just for governments and administrators but for ordinary citizens in the form of such questions as 'What changes shall I campaign for?' If conservatism is a political approach that merits general commendation, and indeed if it is to constitute an ideology as we defined it, it must be understood not merely as giving practical advice to a section of the population but also as having something to say in answer to the political questions which ordinary citizens may need to face.

At this point a conservative might respond by maintaining that what he is offering is advice which is not merely practical, but which is rooted in morality because his concern is the good of the community and hence of all of the individuals within it. So in managing the demands for reform that emanate from others, the conservative statesman is not simply looking after himself or his own social group. His position therefore is more like that of the captain of an aircraft than that of a passenger whose principal concern is only to assure his own safety.

This argument can be understood in more abstract philosophical terms. Kant claimed that all morality, including political morality, must give rise not to *hypothetical* but to *categorical* imperatives. For an agent to act in accordance with a categorical rather than a hypothetical imperative, he must act according to a rule which he desires should apply universally.[7] Modern philosophers do not generally agree that Kant's doctrine of the categorical imperative in fact represents the last word in moral philosophy. One reason is that we cannot apply the doctrine without solving the by now familiar problem of how we formulate the rule which is to be universalized. Thus there may be moral positions which pass the Kantian test but are incompatible with one another. Another source of difficulty is that the stress on universality indicates a controversial commitment to standards of morality which are supposed to apply equally not only to individuals who occupy different positions within a society but to all societies. But whatever the limitations of the Kantian doctrine, we can see that it is an effective weapon in argument against any purely reactive political theory.

Why is this so? A purely reactive conservatism in effect divides people into two classes whom we can label *the privileged* and *the subjects*. Consider the situation of a subject who demands a reason why he should accept a position in which authority and responsibility are to be entrusted to the privileged. A purely reactive conservatism has nothing to say in answer to such an enquirer because although it is seeking to *manage* any demands that he might make, it is not addressing him at all. Instead it patronizes him by treating him as someone who does not need to understand what is going on, just as a doctor patronizes a patient when she prescribes a placebo. In effect a purely reactive conservatism means that the subjects are denied equal membership of the community within which policies require to be justified. Purely reactive conservatism offers no reason why subjects should support it. The position here differs from the case in which a liberal defends his position by invoking deontological assumptions which others reject. In the case of reactive conservatism it is not that the process of rational argument eventually breaks down, but that it never gets started because the subjects are not treated as partners in a rational dialogue. So the Kantian move illustrates that conservatism of this kind involves a rejection of rational political debate.

The conclusion to be drawn from this is not that conservatism is untenable, but that it is a mistake for conservatives to argue in purely reactive terms. The reactive element within conservatism has to be seen as derived from values that can be recommended to all within a community. The conservative thus needs to find an appropriate description of his political approach that will meet the Kantian test. We should, I suggest, understand the conservative message as 'Act in accordance with the settled values and expectations of your community.' Because the nation is conceived as an organic community, different individuals will have different social roles and different things will be expected of different individuals. So the privileged are urged to find ways of managing the demands for change which emanate from others. This they may do through a judicious combination of firmness and a willingness to act on the principle of *'noblesse oblige'*.

But what about those who are not privileged? We have already seen that according to Burke the good life for them is realized when they are 'protected, satisfied, laborious and obedient'. Since it is for others to protect them, the Burkean message to them is that they should be satisfied, laborious and obedient. But being satisfied is a matter of emotional disposition. Once those without privileges seriously contemplate other possibilities, they may find that they cannot readily be satisfied with a situation in which others are permanently privileged? For as long as they can believe that the unity of the nation is not a sham and that the difference between those in authority and themselves is a natural one, perhaps they can contentedly sing the old Victorian hymn

> The rich man in his castle,
> The poor man at his gate,
> God made them high and lowly,
> And ordered his estate.

But if it should cross their minds that perhaps they are being exploited, then even the risks of insecurity and instability may seem worth taking if there is a prospect of improving conditions for themselves and their families. Our view of the nature of traditional conservatism should perhaps be that a widespread interest in political philosophy, leading to a demand for the justification of conservatism itself, is an indication of circumstances in which conservative principles may not be appropriate.

Conservatism and Maximizing Happiness

We have seen that Burke wished people to be satisfied and was concerned by the terrible consequences of the French Revolution, and that more recent conservatives, like Hogg, attached value to the social consequences of religion. This might lead us to wonder whether conservatism itself should be seen as a product of utilitarianism. There are two possible questions here. The first is whether clear-thinking conservatives have to base their political approach on an appeal to maximizing happiness. The second question is whether clear-thinking utilitarians have to be politically conservative.

We are already in a position to suggest a negative answer to the first question. Suppose for the sake of argument that the conservative values of continuity, order and stability do in fact serve to maximize the general happiness. In these circumstances the utilitarian ethic would indeed lead to conservative politics. However, although in those circumstances we would expect all politically committed utilitarians to be conservatives, we would not expect all conservatives who are interested in moral philosophy to be utilitarians. We have already noted that rational argument about moral issues can only arise once we make some assumption which is foundational in the sense of being prior to argument. So we cannot preclude the possibility, even if we think that conservative values do serve to maximize happiness, that some conservatives would prefer to appeal to the intrinsic value of continuity, stability and order.

But it is the second question which is philosophically the more interesting. What makes it so is not the historical evidence which might be adduced for and against the view that continuity, order and stability make for increased happiness, but what it tells us about the banality of seeking to answer fundamental political questions by the simple application of such an abstract general principle as that of utility.

Conservatism, as we have seen, places great value on each person acting in accord with the settled values and expectations of the community. These values and expectations are of course those of the individuals who make up the community, but these individuals are influenced by the prevailing social *mores*. In a settled and stable society children have a structured social environment at home, at school, at play and at worship. Although this is not the whole story, we may presume that one important constituent factor in determining whether an individual's life is happy will be the extent of the fit between that person's aspirations and the expectations of the community. If one aspires to a life in which one cultivates a knowledge of fine wines, it is much better to live in France or indeed any Western country than in an Islamic society. But of course stable Islamic societies are unlikely to contain significant numbers of frustrated wine experts. The point is that it is absurd to consider whether the preservation of a given set of social arrangements will increase the happiness of a community unless we already know something about the identity of its members.

Imagine a utilitarian who in earlier days might have been arguing for women to be permitted equal opportunity to pursue a professional career. One can imagine that in a male-dominated society, there would be many conservatively disposed women who would have been content to function as housewives and mothers in such a society. Such women might have been not merely uninterested, but even hostile to a proposal that they should have equal career opportunities, because they might have perceived that this would create a climate of opinion in which it would be harder for them to lead the kind of life to which they were accustomed. If the utilitarian were confronted with evidence that indicated that this way of thinking was widespread, would we expect her to change her position? The answer is that we would not necessarily do so. We might expect her to argue that these attitudes were themselves the product of a male-dominated society and, together with others of a like mind, to attempt to 'raise the consciousness' of her sisters. If she was successful in raising feminist consciousness amongst other women and in securing the removal of the career barriers, we would expect that those women whose consciousness had been 'raised' would be happier than if the barriers had not been removed. Moreover we might expect that the removal of the barriers would itself have a further effect in helping to produce the conditions in which more women think in career terms and reject the traditional matrimonial and domestic role. Consequently, some time after the changes have been made, we might well be confident that most women would be not merely unhappy but outraged at any proposal to return to the old ways.

The point to which I wish to draw attention is that there is no incompatibility between it being the case that at the outset women would have been made unhappy by the changes and it also being true that subsequently they would be unhappy about the prospect of reversing the changes. There is no puzzle about this. It is simply that the two groups of women are different. I am not referring here to differences in the physical composition of the two populations, but am drawing attention to the fact that the personalities of the women will have been moulded and altered by the change in consciousness and expectations. So although we may ask which situation leads to women being happier, we can only answer the question by focusing on particular women, about whom we have particular knowledge or make particular assumptions and to whom we attribute particular aspirations. So one can argue about restrictions of career opportunities for women on the basis of fairness or perhaps of what is a more natural existence for a woman, or whether the objectives of those women whose consciousness has been 'raised' are more authentic than the more homely ones of women of earlier generations, but one cannot simply invoke utilitarianism in order to arbitrate between two radically different conceptions of how life ought to be led.

A similar point holds in regard to the attempt to argue for a particular conception of community by appealing to the general happiness. Just as feminists think it desirable that women should have aspirations which lead them to resent restrictions on their career opportunities and seek to promote a climate in which they do have such aspirations, so conservatives think it desirable that people should be content to lead lives within the prevailing values and expectations and seek to defend an institutional structure which helps to bring it about that they are so content. But utilitarianism cannot adjudicate between liberal individualism and the conservative conception of community, for what makes people happy is itself a reflection of the assumptions they make about the good life. The difficulty of constructing a good utilitarian case for conservatism is more indicative of the deficiency of utilitarianism than of conservatism.

Further Reading

Precisely because conservatism chooses not to emphasize the importance of rational argument, there is much less published literature about conservative theory than about liberal or socialist theory. There is a good discussion of Burke in M. Freeman, *Edmund Burke and the Critique of Political Radicalism* (Oxford: Basil Blackwell, 1980), and a clear discussion of conservative principles in P. Norton and A. Aughey, *Conservatives and Conservatism* (London: Temple Smith, 1981), chapter 1. For a discussion of different variations on the conservative theme and the development of conservatism in the twentieth century, see N.

O'Sullivan, *Conservatism* (London: Dent, 1976). In addition readers may be interested in the chapters on conservatism in Goodwin, *Using Political Ideas* and Graham, *Politics in its Place*, both of which were cited at the end of chapter 6.

Part IV
Socialism

12

Marxism

In chapter 6 I urged readers to reject the assumption that each or any of the principal positions we are considering has just one 'true' form. This caution is especially relevant to the case of socialism, because of the historical tendency for many professed socialists to seek to identify traitors in their midst. Perhaps the explanation for this predilection lies in the emphasis that many socialists have sought to place on unity within their own ranks. Whatever the reason, the bitterness of divisions such as those between the followers of Stalin and of Trotsky and also those between supporters and opponents of the view that socialism can be realized through gradual evolution within the framework of existing Western constitutional systems has led to much sterile debate about the defining characteristics of 'true' socialism. Possibly the most cynical input into this definitional debate was Herbert Morrison's suggestion that socialism is what a Labour Government does.

Participants in a political struggle often have good reason to emphasize even small disagreements, because their prospects of success may well be frustrated by the activities of those who derive support from the same section(s) of the community. Observers however need to stand back from the heat that is generated so that they do not overlook what political opponents may have in common. I shall not therefore be seeking to adjudicate doctrinal disputes about the meaning of socialism. If my principal interest was to write about the definition of socialism, I would be arguing, along lines similar to those propounded by R. N. Berki, that we should avoid any formula which purports to specify a list of necessary and jointly sufficient conditions of socialism, but instead seek to draw out a number of beliefs which are broadly characteristic of socialism.[1] I shall however also follow David Miller in presuming that two of these elements are especially central.[2] In particular I take socialists to be committed in some degree to a conception of economic equality. It will however be recalled from chapter 2 that talk about equality, at least until some detail is provided, is somewhat unenlightening. I shall also consider socialist concerns with the quality of life.

It will be recalled that my chief concern is not that of contributing to a debate on the correct definition of various ideological positions, but to show how different positions give rise to the possibility of rational argument. So I shall not be offering a taxonomy of socialism and I shall discuss just two of the differing versions of socialism. I intend to look at Marxism, as advocated by Marx himself rather than by twentieth-century Marxists. I shall also look at what I propose to call *constitutional socialism*. This description is intended to designate the approach of those who have claimed to be pursuing socialist objectives, whilst accepting the legal and constitutional framework of Western democracies. This position is often referred to by its adherents as 'democratic socialism'. I have not used this description because the concept of democracy, as we noted in chapter 2, is itself highly problematic. The immediate point of our discussion of both kinds of socialism will be to demonstrate that in both cases adherents are committed to eminently contestable empirical claims and to an equally contestable conception of community.

Marxism, Technology and History

(Communist) society regulates the general production and thus makes it possible for me to do one thing today and another tomorrow, to hunt in the morning, fish in the afternoon, rear cattle in the evening, criticize after dinner . . . without ever becoming hunter, fisherman, cowherd, or critic.
                                        Marx, *The German Ideology*

If socialism can mean different things to different people, it might be observed that the same applies to Marxism. Partly this is because it is often thought to incorporate not only Marx's own ideas, and those of his collaborator Engels, but also the ideas propounded by many later writers who have seen themselves as followers of Marx. Partly it is also because Marx's own writings have been the subject of radically different interpretations. In what follows, I shall be concerned only with positions taken by Marx himself, as I interpret him. Since the main point here as ever is not Marxian scholarship but an illustration of the extent to which different political positions give rise to the possibility of rational argument, I shall not seek to justify the correctness of my interpretation.

What makes Marx unusual among political theorists is the degree of emphasis that he gives to the explanation of how particular kinds of social arrangement have arisen. His theory of society maintains that political life is determined by economic circumstances which are independent of the wills of individuals. Those who think that the case for socialism can be advanced by appeals to the consciences of people who profit from capitalism are seen as utopians whistling in the wind. Marx did agree, for reasons which we shall discuss below, that capitalism was a system in which many were consigned to leading wretched lives, but he thought it essential that this perception must be combined with an objective understanding of how change is to be brought about. In other words what Marx thought was needed was a scientific theory of history.

The key element for understanding any society, in Marx's view, is the level of technology employed in the process of production. In any society people have physical needs for food, warmth and shelter. In primitive societies where men are hunter-gatherers, tools are rudimentary and small groups are self-sufficient.[3] Progress comes as the business of production becomes more effectively organized. Warmth and shelter can be more reliably provided when permanent accommodation is built. This can only be done when there is a secure expectation that there will be a sufficient and dependable food supply. This in turn requires the cultivation of the land. All of these things are done more effectively as the technology of production and distribution become more advanced.

For the utilization of any technology, three factors are essential. The first is the existence of what Marx calls *forces of production*, namely the necessary raw materials and implements, such as tools and machinery, which are needed to process the materials. So for example agriculture is impossible in the absence of fertile soil, and fishing cannot be effectively carried out without the assistance of such devices as boats, nets and hooks. Secondly men must have an understanding of how these forces can be harnessed to the task of production. Coal, fertile soil, uranium, are for example all useless to nomadic hunters. In short any material force of production is only of value to those who know how to deploy it. Thirdly men require the power to extract these forces from the environment and harness them in the productive process. Thus fertile land can only be exploited by those who have the physical strength to till the soil or manage the cattle that graze the land, or of course the social power to get others to do it for them. As our technology becomes more sophisticated, we may need less physical strength than previously, but some physical power is still needed to make use of the machinery.

Compared with other species, man is held to be a reflective and creative animal who fulfils himself best when he is engaged in pursuits other than the satisfaction of purely physical needs. So mathematicians, poets, and even craftsmen express themselves imaginatively in ways that cannot be seen as simply functional. This creativity can however only be fully realized in an environment which is free from the pressure of urgent physical need. An artist for example cannot paint with total freedom and spontaneity if he is at all times concerned about having to sell his work in order to eat. Because we best fulfil ourselves in pursuing activities that are not directly concerned with the satisfaction of physical need, we are always receptive to ideas which make the productive process more efficient. Therefore there is a long-term historical trend for our technology to develop.

The development of technology is connected, in Marx's view, to the phenomenon of class. Once mankind has progressed beyond the primitive era, developing technology gives rise to an increasing division of labour in which specialized roles are carried out by those who have particular access to the technology or particular skills in utilizing it. The important division in a class society is identified as being between those who have effective control of the prevailing technology and those who do not. The former group, who at different points of history can be characterized as slave-owners, feudal lords, or industrial capitalists, will dominate those who do not, namely the slaves, serfs or workers. All aspects of the life of the dominant class reflect the fact that they are the dominant class, just as all aspects of the life of a dominated class reflect the fact that others control the technology. Social and political institutions, laws, schools, churches, moral and philosophical systems all evolve, according to the theory, so as to reinforce the power of the dominant class.

Why then does anything ever change? Marx's answer invokes the continuing development of technology. To be effectively and efficiently harnessed different kinds of technology require different forms of social organization. As Marx put it in a famous phrase in *The Poverty of Philosophy*, 'the hand-mill gives you society with the feudal lord; the steam-mill, society with the industrial capitalist'.[4] Hand-mills are such that they can readily be controlled by the feudal lords, whereas steam-mills require the existence of factories and coal-mines as well as a labour force educated to operate them. Marx claims that when one class has control of society, it will seek to promote all and only those technological developments that reinforce its control and to suppress any radically new technology which, if developed, would threaten the continuation of the kind of life to which its members have become accustomed. But human innovativeness cannot be perfectly controlled and the development of a new technology which will radically improve the business of production and offer an improvement in the living conditions of those who are not members of the dominant class cannot forever be prevented. Moreover once it begins to develop, its growth will be accompanied by the emergence of a new class of people who are specially adept in making use of the new technology. When one controlling class displaces another, what happens is not just a change of regime but a wholesale social revolution in which all aspects of society reflect the interest of those who have gained power. Marx's example *par excellence* is the destruction of feudal society in the wake of the Industrial Revolution. What occurred was a massive migration from rural areas into towns and cities, the replacement of the traditional extended family units by small nuclear families (i.e. just parents and children) which could readily be accommodated in the small houses that were built in enormous numbers within easy reach of the factories, the development of a legal system which emphasized the protection of property and the enforcement of contracts, a limited widening of the franchise which reduced the power of the nobility and facilitated the election of governments committed to the defence of capitalist interests, and the evolution of an ethic which stressed the merits of enterprise, self-reliance and hard work.

It is important to grasp however that although Marx sees development in technology as the key to change, he does not think that major structural change always occurs as an immediate response to such development. He believes that for any kind of technology there is an optimum form of social organization, but concedes that once a new technology is introduced, there may be a long period before that particular kind of social organization evolves. So there can be transitional phases and indeed it is Marx's view that capitalism is such a transitional phase. Although Marx held that the development of modern industrial technology gives initial control to the capitalist class, he also maintained that capitalism was an inherently unstable system.

From Capitalism to Socialism

The success of capitalism, Marx holds, requires the stimulation of demand for the goods which capitalists can supply, which means that the working class who constitute the majority must have the resources to buy these goods. However since the individual interest of each capitalist is the maximization of profit, he will seek to extract the largest amount of productive work from his employees for the smallest amount of pay. To do otherwise would make him uncompetitive with other capitalists. The consequence is that individual capitalists behave in a way that ultimately spells the destruction of capitalism. For a long time this is not evident because colonization and military conquest enable markets to expand. But, since markets cannot expand indefinitely, capitalism cannot endure indefinitely. This is what Marx means by his prediction that capitalism will be destroyed by its internal contradictions. In his view a number of factors combine to ensure that the ground becomes increasingly fertile for socialists to persuade workers that capitalism can and should be overthrown. One such consideration is the fact that the capitalist's need for productive efficiency leads to unpleasant, dangerous working conditions for his employees. Another is that economic competition between capitalists is held to create a situation in which workers constantly face unemployment or the prospect of becoming unemployed. As new markets become harder to find so also more and more capitalists are driven out of business, and the proportion of workers to capitalists in the population increases.

Moreover the large-scale organization of production ensures that workers come into daily contact with many who share their misery and thus facilitates the development of a shared consciousness. When working-class consciousness eventually matures, the workers finally succeed in taking over control of the forces of production from the capitalists. Technological change does not then come to a halt, but because all now share in the control of resources, there is no longer any particular social group whose members can use new technology specifically for their own rather than the common advantage. Eventually a communist society will emerge, in which political coercion is no longer needed, and which will function in accordance with the famous distributive principle cited in the *Critique of the Gotha Programme*, namely 'from each according to his ability, to each according to his need',[5] and individuals will conduct themselves as described in the passage already quoted from *The German Ideology*. There will then be a form of social organization which is appropriate to modern technology.

The Marxist account of history may seem descriptive rather than evaluative. We could readily imagine someone being convinced that a capitalist society can never be in stable equilibrium and that the kind of society Marx envisages is inevitable, without approving of the prospect. Before we consider the extent to which Marx makes a case for socialism, as opposed to a case for the inevitability of socialism, it is important to be clear about one aspect of his theory of history which has been the source of much confusion.

Marxism and Determinism

Some people have thought that Marx was committed to a fatalistic vision of man, according to which our actions must always be determined by mysterious economic forces even when we are totally unaware of them. Marx's account of history is thus sometimes seen as a threat to freedom, not in the political sense in which freedom is opposed to oppression, but in the sense that our supposed ability to take decisions and make choices turns out to be illusory. If socialism is inevitable anyway, there might seem little point in arguing about whether it is our duty to work to achieve it.

The pessimistic thought that human freedom, or free will, may be no more than a cherished illusion is often evoked by attempts to explain the world. It is prompted for some by the belief that every physical event has a prior cause and that human actions are themselves the product of physical events in the form of electrical activity within the brain. For others it is occasioned by Freudian psychology with its suggestion that our behaviour is the product of motives of which we are unconscious. The possibility of human freedom has also been a problem for many theologians who believed that the world was the product of an omnipotent God, and who wondered how one could then hold individuals responsible for their own behaviour.

These are important philosophical issues. Do we have reason for supposing that there is a sense in which determinism is true? If so, does this mean that the idea of human freedom must be rejected and that we should think of human beings rather as if they are dancers whose every step has been mysteriously and meticulously choreographed in advance? These issues are ones that I mention here because it is often thought that Marxism is in this sense strongly deterministic. I shall not here pursue the issue of whether these other forms of explanation pose a threat to human freedom but I suggest that nothing in Marx's explanations commits him to viewing human beings as choreographed dancers. Although Marx believed that man's options were constrained by his historical circumstances, he emphatically rejected the suggestion that they could make no choices for themselves. He wrote that 'men make their own history but they do not make it just as they please; they do not make it under circumstances chosen by themselves, but under circumstances directly encountered, given and transmitted from the past'.[6] The reason why human freedom is not threatened by Marx's attempt to treat history as a science is because, like many scientific enterprises, Marx's account of society operates on a 'macro' level and not a 'micro' level. Consider again the evolutionary arguments of Darwinian biology. Darwin explains how some animals have an advantage over other members of the same species, which will enable them to be more effective in finding food or attracting prospective mates or defending themselves against predators, and will thus make it likely that they will have greater success in procreation. Because progeny tend to resemble their parents, the advantage will tend to spread throughout the population. Notice that nothing in this explanation leads us to suppose that any given animal in the advantaged category will inevitably breed successfully or that one in the disadvantaged category will inevitably fail to do so. So an explanation which we may find compelling at a 'macro' level may leave open the question of what happens at the 'micro' level.

Marx maintains that something similar applies in history. Suppose that we ask why socialists cannot prevail by persuading capitalists of the immorality of the private ownership of the means of production. A Marxist might point out that if an individual capitalist is persuaded, he can respond only by going out of business. The option of paying his workers above the market rate is not viable in the long term, because such a capitalist will become uncompetitive.[7] But in that case the capitalist's market share will simply be taken over by someone who has no compunction about using his ownership of the means of production to make a profit.

Thus, no individual capitalist has it within his power to abolish capitalism, but this does not conflict with Marx's view of capitalism as a man-made economic system.

If Marx's view is correct, then economic systems are independent of the will of individuals, but not independent of human will. His position is that capitalism cannot be defeated as the result of any decisions of individual capitalists. This does not however mean that it could survive a simultaneous decision by all capitalists to abandon ownership of the means of production. But since there is no framework which can lead us to expect such an event, Marx thought that we could safely discount it. Here he is operating with a conception of social science as concerned with the wider, and generally unintended, consequences of human action. Although, as will be suggested, there is a weakness in Marx's account of human motivation, it is quite wrong to suppose that he thought that human beings were but the playthings of impersonal economic forces.

Marx and Morality

But even if we grant that Marx is not in this sense a determinist, nevertheless some think that he analyses morality as no more than a product of the economic structure of society. Is this view correct? It is true that in Marx's view morality in capitalist society normally reflects the interests of the capitalist or bourgeois class. Not only does he think that members of the capitalist class tend to subscribe to moral beliefs which reinforce capitalism by justifying their own power, but also that they use this power to disseminate their values to members of the working class, so that they too, at least until the capitalist structure begins to crumble, are likely to make moral judgements which reflect the interests of the bourgeoisie. This situation changes as capitalism enters the throes of its final crisis and the workers become conscious of their own class interest, but even here the moral judgements made by the workers are class-based. So social morality always reflects a class interest, and Marx therefore may be thought to be arguing only that the destruction of capitalism is a good thing for the workers, rather than that it is something which *ought*, independently of class interest, to be promoted.

This interpretation of Marx is certainly nearer the mark than the attribution to him of the view that human beings are but hapless pawns of economic forces, but it is still not correct. We have noted that Marx the social scientist was concerned with explaining the prevalent features of a society. So he does indeed think of the *predominant* morality within a class as always a class morality. He believes that it is always possible to explain, by reference to the economic structure of a society, why the prevalent moral beliefs within a class have the character they do. But it does not follow from this that all morality is based on class interest. To suppose otherwise is to fail to realize that Marx's explanations are intended to apply only at the 'macro' level. Though it was important to Marx that he and his supporters could present social-ism to the workers as something which would be a good thing *for them*, he also thought that the attractions of socialism were ones which could be recommended to a wider public. In other words he makes a moral case for socialism. If this were not so, we should have to wonder whether he thought that there was any reason for middle-class intellectuals, like Engels and indeed Marx himself, to lend their support to the socialist movement.

Another reason why Marx is sometimes interpreted as a prophet rather than an advocate is that he was interested principally in changing things rather than in talking about the need for change. People who want to achieve results, whether they are generals fighting wars, politicians fighting elections, or boxing managers or sporting coaches, habitually make upbeat pronouncements about the prospects of success. Marx's frequent references to the inevitability of socialism can be seen in this way. But such talk about the inevitability of victory does not preclude maintaining that there is a moral case for this change. As a practical man Marx did not think he could promote socialism by convincing capitalists of the error of their ways. So he did not engage in casuistry about the immorality of capitalism, and declared contemptuously that 'communists do not preach morality at all'.[8]

To doubt the efficacy of moral argument is not the same as rejecting morality. There is a difference between believing that one can make a case for the acceptance of a proposition which ought to be accepted by all rational persons, and believing that everyone can in fact be persuaded of the merits of this case. That Galileo bowed to pressure and renounced his belief in the Copernican System is an indication that he realized that he could not persuade everyone in a world dominated by the power of the medieval church of the truth of his astronomical opinions, but it is not an indication that he thought he lacked good arguments for these opinions. Similarly the fact that Marx was scathing about the activity of moralizing and anxious to appeal to the class-interest of the workers in the destruction of capitalism gives us no reason to suppose that he lacked moral opinions. Indeed we have good reason to believe that he did have moral opinions since he explicitly writes of 'the moral degradation resulting from the capitalist exploitation of the labour of women and children'.[9] We still however need to see what Marx's moral case for socialism amounts to, and how it relates to his supposedly objective account of social history.

Marxism and Human Nature

We observed earlier that the key to Marx's theory of history lies in the idea of technological development which is itself rooted in two generalizations about man. These generalizations, namely that man is innovative and that he fulfils himself in creative activities that are not geared to the satisfaction of pressing physical need, might be taken to constitute a significant part of a theory of human nature. Marxists sometimes resist this suggestion, because they believe that behavioural characteristics are affected by the economic structure of society and will therefore be different in different kinds of society. So for example they suppose that man's competitiveness is not a universal characteristic but one which reflects the antagonistic nature of capitalist society. To that extent they believe that man's nature will be transformed in a socialist society. But this does not imply that man's nature is completely plastic or that it is impossible to make any trans-historical or trans-cultural generalizations about human beings. Indeed it is precisely the temptation to suppose that the two generalizations just mentioned apply universally which gives plausibility to Marx's claim that there is a historical tendency for continuing technological development. So Marx's whole theory of history is underpinned by these empirical claims about man's nature, or to use Marx's own term, man's 'species-being'.[10]

It is important to realize that Marx does not content himself with a neutral description of man based solely on empirical observation and a neutral study of history. His theory of human nature is evaluative and not simply descriptive. In fact this is usually the case whenever someone talks about human nature or what is natural for man, and is in contrast with talk about what is 'natural' in the case of inanimate objects. Consider the following propositions:

(A) It is natural for ice-cubes to melt in a warm atmosphere.

and

(B) It is natural for adults to comfort a crying baby.

Proposition (A) is entirely descriptive. If on a single occasion we found that an ice-cube did not melt in a warm atmosphere, we would say that this refuted proposition (A). We would *not* consider the possibility that proposition (A) is true but that the ice-cube was responding *un*naturally. In the case of proposition (B), however, we certainly do not think that the behaviour in question amounts to a universal rule, and so we allow the possibility of 'unnatural' behaviour. But the difference is not simply between a universal claim and a probabilistic one. If for example we claimed that it was unnatural for a girl of 12 to have no social life but to train for eight hours every day in order to try to become an Olympic swimming champion, it would be inferred that we thought that this behaviour was not just unusual but bad for her. If behaviour is unnatural, it is not consonant with the flourishing of the individual who engages in it. In this example the girl may be content, at least in the sense that she may attain what she most wants, namely an Olympic gold medal, but if our claim is right her prospects of a good life are diminished.

Some people will be suspicious of such talk. How, they might wonder, can someone else say that an individual is not flourishing or not having a good life, when that person is getting what she wants? Anyone making such a judgement, it may be objected, has to specify their criteria of a good life and tell us how they are to be justified. This is no easy undertaking, but at least there is the possibility of citing some evidence against the assumption that the good life simply consists in getting as much as possible of what one wants. Take the case of a 'yuppy' who earns enormous sums in his early twenties by sitting in front of a computer screen, with a bank of telephones by his side, and who constantly and instantly makes deals with people he never meets. He may quickly become wealthy and acquire all the material possessions to which he aspires. Insofar as his wants are satisfied he is content, but does he flourish? In order to answer this question, we might wish to have further information. We might want to know whether he looks happy, whether he makes heavy use of stimulants such as drugs or alcohol, whether he sleeps well, whether he seems able to relax, and whether he develops high blood pressure or other signs of stress.

So to say that behaviour is unnatural is normally to commit ourselves to the value judgement that there is something wrong with it, and we may be able to cite evidence that those who engage in it do not flourish. We can see that someone who asserts proposition (B) is indicating their view that there is something wrong with the person who does not comfort the crying baby. My suggestion is that Marx appeals in a similar way to an evaluative conception of human nature.

His technique owes much to Aristotle, whom Marx studied as a young doctoral student. There are two related dimensions to the Aristotelian method. The first is the emphasis on essence. Aristotle holds that in order to understand any object, we must abstract those of its properties which are essential to its nature from those which are merely accidental. So a particular man (understood in the sense of a member of the species *homo sapiens* rather than a person of male gender) may also be a doctor, but he can retain his identity as a man whilst ceasing to be a doctor. Thus being a doctor is an accidental, not an essential, property of an individual man. In order to know what are the essential properties of a man we have to know what makes him a man *rather* than some other kind of object. So we can for example exclude what Aristotle calls 'the life of nutrition and growth' from the essence of a man because these are also characteristic of plants and 'the life of perception' because this is shared by horses and oxen.[11]

The second Aristotelian tendency is to seek to define the essence of an object in terms of its function. Aristotle himself says that 'all things derive their essential character from their function and their capacity'.[12] So what we want to know about a bag is that it is to be used for carrying small objects, whereas in the case of a chair we need to know that it is suitable for sitting on. With this information we make judgements about whether a bag or a chair is a good one.

Marx's Aristotelian method means that his account of man is based on an answer to the question, 'What is man's characteristic excellence?' The answer, which is given synoptically in the quotation from the *The German Ideology* in chapter 12 emphasizes not simply what is characteristically human but what is distinctively human. So one reason why Marx is scathing about capitalism is that it is, he thinks, an economic system which constrains the workers to seek satisfaction not in creative activity, but in the fulfilment of their purely biological needs, in other words in just the kind of behavioural traits they share with animals, as opposed to the ones that distinguish them from animals. Workers carry out productive activity but in circumstances which stress the importance of productive efficiency rather than the stimulus of creativity. Also since what the workers produce is appropriated by those who control the working environment, work takes on the character of a drudge, undertaken not for its own sake but for the sake of the wages that will enable the workers and their families to survive. That men are cut off from fulfilling their natural potential, the phenomenon that Marx characterizes as alienation, constitutes in his view a reduction of man to the level of animals. Capitalism is thus held to be dehumanizing.

Marx's writings are then an exercise not merely in social history but also in moral criticism. He does not condemn individual capitalists for the existence of capitalism, but he does condemn the immorality of capitalism. And he does therefore need to offer some argument for the moral superiority of socialism. As we have seen, he is committed to the view that economic circumstances are such as to preclude the possibility of his convincing the mass of capitalists of the moral superiority of socialism, and as a man of action he had little time for moralizing. But his writings contain the basis of a moral argument. According to Marx everyone in capitalist society, including each and every capitalist, is cut off from the possibility of self-realization. But it is precisely because the destruction of the class system will in Marx's view lead to self-realization for all, that, once the revolution has taken proper root and the traces of capitalism have been removed, people will thereafter be content to live in communist society. We observed above that people can be content without flourishing. But we can at least presume that if they are flourishing they will be content, and this is why Marx views communism as the ultimate form of society, which, once established, will never be abandoned. So Marx's moral commitment to an evaluative conception of human nature plays a crucial role in his political theory. His account of capitalism is not merely descriptive but implies the moral superiority of socialism. Marx portrays socialism not merely as something which is claimed to be a natural development from capitalism, but as something to be welcomed as a liberation of the human spirit.

13

Arguing about Marxism

Marx's Descriptive Thesis

My account of Marx has brought out two crucial aspects of his political theory. These are the descriptive thesis that capitalism will give way to socialism, and the evaluative thesis that the good life is to be found in creative activity which is performed in an environment free from the pressure of immediate physical need. Perhaps because all have been willing to agree that Marx is committed to a descriptive thesis, more attention has been given by philosophers to this dimension of his work than to the evaluative thesis. The most prevalent criticism, memorably put forward by Karl Popper,[1] is that Marx's claim to have put the study of history on to a scientific footing, on the basis of which we can confidently predict the advent of socialism, is bogus. This criticism must seen in the context of Popper's interest in the status of scientific beliefs. His target was the view that the role of science is to establish laws of nature which unfailingly govern the workings of the universe. The problem with universal laws is that they are not merely propositions about what happens, but also what always has happened and what always will happen. However, as David Hume had pointed out in the eighteenth century, we can never deduce anything about what will happen from knowledge of what has happened.[2] It may be sensible to assume that the future will resemble the past but this must always remain an unproven assumption.

The upshot of Hume's point is that we never can deduce any universal laws whatever. No amount of observations of water freezing at 0° Celsius in conditions of normal atmospheric pressure can ever be a basis for the inference that water always will freeze in these conditions. Should we then abandon the view that science is an intellectually rigorous activity? One unsatisfactory move was to insist that science was properly concerned with establishing universal laws, but to concede that its methods were not rigorously deductive. Instead scientific reasoning was held by some to be characterized by a probabilistic form of reasoning which was based on the assumption that the past would be a reliable guide to the future. This avowedly non-deductive method was labelled *inductive*, but this should not obscure the fact that so-called inductive reasoning is simply deductively invalid.

What Popper saw however is that we need not abandon the view that science is a rational and intellectually rigorous activity. Instead we have to abandon the view that the business of science is to establish universal laws, since universal generalizations about what always happens can never be established. What can be established however with total intellectual rigour is the falsity of some such generalizations. The reason is that although no amount of observation of events unfolding in accordance with a generaliz-ation will establish that the generalization is universally true, a single instance of an event which defies a universal generalization will show that generalization to be false.

So for Popper the character of scientific explanations is that they are *falsifiable*. This means that any scientific theory must give rise to predictions which put that theory at risk, i.e. predic-tions which, if false, will be seen to be false and whose falsification amounts to a refutation of the theory. Take as an example the explanation for the melting of a lump of ice, namely that it is subjected to an ambient temperature above 0° Celsius. This explanation can readily be tested because it generates predictions like

(A)   If I remove this ice-cube from the freezer and place it on a desk in my warm office, it will immediately start to melt.

If by any chance this prediction was wrong, we would have no trouble observing that it was wrong, and we would have to reconsider our long-held view about the nature of ice.

Notice that the prediction above is different from a rather less precise one which we might have made, namely

(B)   If I remove this ice-cube from the freezer and place it on a desk in my warm office, it will eventually melt.

The point about this latter prediction is that although it is *verifiable*, in that we know exactly what possible observations might demonstrate its truth, there are no observations which could conclusively demonstrate its falsity. Because such a prediction neither has implications for what is supposed to happen immediately nor suggests any time by which anything is supposed to have happened, we can say that it is unfalsifiable. There are only two possible verdicts when we have subjected this latter prediction to a 'test'. At the time of the test it has either turned out to be true, or it has not yet turned out to be true. In the latter case a stubborn defender of the prediction can always say that it will still turn out eventually to have been true. The 'test' for this prediction turns out to have been one that it might have passed but could not possibly have failed. The proposition amounts to a *safe prophecy*, not because we confidently expect it to be borne out, but because there is no possibility of refutation. In this sense, it would be equally safe to predict that some day the United States will defeat England at cricket. According to Popper, scientists must do something riskier than subject their conclusions to unfailable 'tests'. Their business is to formulate theories which tell us that events we might otherwise have thought possible cannot in fact occur. So their explanations must give rise to risky predictions, not safe prophecies. According to Popper, Marx's supposedly scientific account of history makes just this mistake. The prediction that capitalism eventually gives rise to socialism is a safe prophecy, so that any country which had a capitalist economy at one point in history has at a later time either developed a socialist economy or not yet developed a socialist economy.

Though philosophers are now generally agreed that Popper is right to see falsifiability as a criterion for science, his argument that Marxism is unscientific is a little hasty, though it points us in a relevant direction. Certainly we cannot assume that we have a safe warrant for the projection of long-term historical trends into the future, because statements of long-term trends are unlike statements of scientific laws in that a failure of future events to conform to an alleged trend may be held to have *gone against the trend*, as for example the collapse of share prices in October 1987 went against the long-term trend for equity values to at least keep pace with inflation. Something being shown to go against a trend may be surprising but is different from a demonstration that there is no such trend. So statements of long-term trends are not readily vulnerable to falsification and thus not a basis for forming expectations about what will happen in the future.

Marxian Predictions

However I suggest that it is unfair to cast Marx in the role of someone making unfalsifiable predictions. In fact his predictions are arguably conditional in much the same way as those of orthodox economists. Consider the kind of prediction made by monetarist economists to the effect that printing money to meet wage demands results in inflation in the costs of goods and services. Notice that this prediction is a conditional one. It is not that economists believe that the inflation would occur whatever human beings chose to do. In particular it is recognized that it would not occur if most people decided to put all their extra money away in a box under the bed. In fact we know that some people may initially behave in that way, but what happens is an increase in the amount of money in circulation as other people either spend their extra cash themselves or invest it and thus increase the funds available to others. Since most suppliers of goods and services will choose to increase their prices, both to cover increased wage costs and because they perceive that the market can bear such an increase, those who opt to place the extra money in a box find that they are subject to increasing pressure to draw on these funds or to invest them so as to receive a return on the money. So the prediction is not a prophecy of what is bound to happen willy-nilly, but of what can be expected to happen given that a large number of people will be motivated to act in pursuit of their economic self-interest. Economists do not seek to prove that particular individuals will choose to spend or invest their money rather than put it in a box under the bed, but make conditional predictions which reflect their belief that most people who demand a wage increase will not be inclined to leave that increase in a box. Moreover there are many factors other than the amount of money in circulation which may have an effect on the rate at which people save. These include the perceived quality of goods, whether people expect war to break out, and the expectations that people have about future rates of inflation. Moreover such factors will also affect the time it takes for an increase in the amount of money in circulation to percolate through to prices. So if it is known that a new model of a popular car will become available next year, a significant part of the inflationary effect may be deferred. In consequence no sensible economist will predict that a given percentage increase in the amount of money that is printed will result in a corresponding increase in inflation by a given date.

My suggestion is that Marx's theory of history similarly reflects the assumption that people in a capitalist society will act in self-interested ways. He supposes that the most successful capitalists will be concerned above all with maximizing their profits. Because they will wish to cut unit costs, wages will be low, hours will be long, and money will only be spent on workers' safety if the danger imperils production. Capitalists who did not share these attitudes would come under pressure to conform or to go out of business. Since markets cannot be expanded indefinitely, some capitalists inevitably lose out so that the numerical strength of the working class increases. This happens at the same time as their working conditions and security of employment decline. Without employment workers are faced with the possibility of starvation. Eventually the climate becomes right for the workers to grasp the socialist message that if they unite and expropriate the remaining capitalists, they will succeed in removing the cause of their enduring misery. Once they understand this, they will be motivated to do it. So Marx is making long-term but not unconditional predictions, based on certain assumptions about human motivation.

In assessing this theory of history, we might object that there seem to be few capitalist societies in which there is much sign of an impending socialist revolution. The evidence of 1989 was that it was the economies which had been run on supposedly socialist lines which were disintegrating. Should Marx's predictions, like proposition (B), be rejected as unfalsifiable and hence dogmatic because they lack any implicit time-scale? I suggest that this is not the most appropriate criticism to make of Marx's theory of history. It is certainly true that Marx's prediction of the demise of capitalism is unlike the kinds of prediction which can be derived from theories in physics. There is no Marxian equivalent to predictions of the time of the next high tide or of the time of the next eclipse of the moon. The question however is whether Marx's predictions, like those of economic monetarists, could be viewed not as propositions which constitute a crucial test for the theory, but as expectations which have a reasonable basis in propositions that are falsifiable.

Let us draw an analogy with a prediction that might be made by a fish biologist. Suppose that small amounts of a chemical pollutant have been discharged into a lake inhabited by a particular species of fish, and scientists tell us that the toxicity will take hundreds of years to abate. A biologist may inform us that the substance is damaging to the reproductive capacities of the fish and consequently that, given a continuation of normal fluctuations in the other independent variables that are relevant to the breeding success of the species, they will eventually die out. Unless the level of toxicity is so high that the fish perish at once or none of them can reproduce successfully, he cannot however be expected to give us even an approximate date by which the last fish will have died. Nor can he even be certain that the effect of the pollutant will be a reduction each year in the numbers of fish that would otherwise be spawned, because for a time the damage done to the fish population may be offset by the fact that even greater damage is done to predator or competitor species. But the biologist might still be confident of his prediction because the damage is such that the fish will not be able to breed successfully once other factors cease to be especially favourable.

The prediction is not itself a scientific pronouncement or a biological finding, but it may well be that biology provides good grounds for the prediction. Although the claim that the fish will eventually die out may be unfalsifiable, it might be that it is a reasonable expectation based on propositions which are falsifiable, namely that the current level of toxicity does significant damage to the reproductive capacity of the fish and that this level of toxicity will not significantly decline for hundreds of years. If the fish then increase in number during the next two or three years, the biologist may well be able to explain this as a short-term effect which does no damage to the credibility of his initial prediction. This is not however to admit that the fish biologist's prediction could be defended against any amount of apparent counter-evidence.

I suggest that Marx's prediction of socialism succeeding capitalism can be seen as roughly analogous in form. It can be viewed as rooted in claims, instanced above, about how individual capitalists behave and in particular how they treat members of the working class. These claims, I suggest, are falsifiable. We can examine the amount of money which capitalists choose to spend on the safety of their workforce. We can determine whether the purchasing power of workers increases or decreases over time. We can measure the level of unemployment and determine whether it is rising. Marx allows that the factors which determine economic outcomes are complex, and he can therefore accommodate the fact that capitalism has periods of increasing prosperity. But just as we saw that the plausibility of the fish biologist's prediction could withstand a certain amount of apparent counter-evidence, so in some circumstances it might be reasonable to allow some latitude to the Marxist. If for example we confront the Marxist with evidence that a capitalist economy has been providing increasing prosperity for the workers over a period of years, he may feel able to explain this by showing that it is a consequence of expanding the production of armaments in order to face down a rival power. This can be compared with the period in which the fish thrive, because the pollution first of all takes greater toll of others. In each case what we have to decide is whether the defender of the prediction has a built-in way of dealing with all counter-evidence in which case what we confront is dogmatic prophecy, or whether the handling of the apparent counter-evidence can itself be satisfactorily related to some falsifiable claim.

Unfortunately for Marx's account of history, the failure of capitalism to crumble as predicted cannot be easily accommodated within his theory. There are many respects in which capitalism may be thought to have developed in ways that Marx did not anticipate. In particular the development of the mixed economy, the way in which workers might themselves also become investors through direct share ownership or through pensions schemes, and in which significant economic power might pass to managers may all be seen as salient features of capitalism for which Marx did not allow. I shall focus simply on assumptions he makes about the behaviour of both capitalists and workers. He seeks to draw a conclusion about the economic situation of workers on the basis of how individual rationally self-interested capitalists would treat them. The problem is not that Marx's assumptions about capitalists and workers behave are unfalsifiable, but that they are actually false. In a completely *laissez-faire* economy these suppositions might have proved correct. Imagine a Dickensian society in which domestic heating normally takes the form of coal fires and in which it is permissible to employ young children as chimney sweeps. Someone who was running a chimney-sweeping business could not then readily choose to dispense with child labour, because young children can be paid less than adults and are small enough to climb into the chimneys. For an individual employer child labour is therefore highly cost-efficient. If one individual employer refused to recruit children, he would almost certainly go out of business. In such circumstances we would expect to find that all successful chimney-sweeping businesses make use of child labour. But our circumstances are not ones in which *laissez-faire* applies to the employment of children. Those seeking to employ children in dirty jobs will fall foul of legislation. Moreover employers may well not be opposed to such legislation, provided that they believe that it will be effectively enforced, because they have an assurance that their competitors will not be able to take advantage of child labour.

One of Marx's principal failures is to take due account of the ability of capitalists to combine in defence of capitalism. This they do, not through the way that each chooses to conduct his own business, but through their support for the state. The state may impose safety legislation, restrict working hours, provide medical care and educational opportunities for workers, and undertake any number of activities which will lead workers to be broadly satisfied, or at least less dissatisfied, with the quality of their lives. A substantial amount of the funding for such a state comes from capitalists. Why are they content with such a state, and why do many keenly support political parties committed to a welfare state, or at least one which is much more extensive than the minimal state favoured by Nozick? A possible answer is that if the state can ensure that the general level of welfare is such as to preclude the establishment of a climate in which revolutionary consciousness develops amongst the workers, this is beneficial to the long-term prospects of capitalists themselves. Moreover there is no conflict with the capitalist's individual interest so long as he can be confident that any restrictions apply to his competitors as well as himself. So the situation of workers may not be determined solely by the way in which individual employers choose to treat them. It may also be partly determined by government policy, and capitalists may have an interest in supporting a government which ensures that workers receive better treatment than they would in a completely *laissez-faire* economy. Moreover what I have just described is no mere theoretical possibility. This is precisely what has happened since Marx wrote *Capital*. So although we find much evidence that manufacturers, food producers, airlines and shipping companies have often neglected or sought to evade safety and hygiene regulations, so we also find much evidence that they support the existence of such regulations and attempts by government to enforce them. Thus many oil companies support the phased but mandatory introduction of lead-free petrol, though they showed little interest in marketing it until there were signs that governments were moving in the direction of discouraging the use of leaded petrol.

Just as capitalists have found a way of defending their class interest more effectively than Marx allowed, so workers are less easily able than he assumed to put their alleged class interest above their individual interest. For each worker, participation in a revolutionary struggle is arguably in his class interest, but certainly not in his individual interest. The reason is that each individual significantly increases the risk of getting himself killed by taking part in a revolutionary struggle, whilst only marginally increasing the chance of the revolution succeeding. Nevertheless it might be plausible to suppose that the class interest may predominate in circumstances in which life otherwise seems intolerable. So if for example unemployed workers really are threatened with the prospect of starvation, and if other workers are impoverished and have no job security, they may well feel that they have little to lose and be ready to see themselves principally as members of an oppressed class. But if the state ensures that conditions for the workers and the unemployed are less dire than Marx expected, then members of the working class may have much to lose in the revolutionary struggle. In that case Marxists can have no reason for confidence that they can succeed in sowing the seeds of revolutionary class consciousness. So the trouble with the descriptive thesis is that it is not securely rooted in an understanding of the facts.

Marx's Evaluative Thesis

The foundational belief of Marx's evaluative thesis is constituted by the idea that the good life is one in which, freed from the structural inequalities of capitalism, we can fulfil our distinctively human capacities. Obviously there is scope for debate about the extent to which Marx is correct to suppose that capitalism leads to the frustration of these capacities and socialism to their realization. The first of these questions is closely related to the descriptive thesis we have just discussed. However let us now consider the attractions of aspiring to a life that centres around the fulfilment of our distinctively human capacities.

Notice that Marx's terminology tends to beg the question. He talks of man's 'true nature'[3], and it is from the full realization of this true nature that man is 'alienated' in capitalism. In the *Preface to the Critique of Political Economy*, the destruction of capitalism is described as bringing 'the prehistory of human society to a close'.[4] Talk of *true nature, alienation* and *prehistory* illustrate a commitment to the view that the characteristic behaviour of man in a socialist society is not merely different from his behaviour in a capitalist society but qualitatively superior. It reflects the assumption that our distinctive human qualities, which Marx believes will be expressed in socialist communities, are more authentic than those we share with non-human animals.

There are two points to be made about this assumption. The first concerns Marx's view of other species. The idea that human fulfilment lies in the exercise of distinctively human capacities is more intuitively attractive if we suppose that non-human animals are all brutish, instinctive creatures lacking consciousness. But this view of non-human animals has ceased to be fashionable. However imperfectly we understand other species, many non-human animals appear to manifest great concern for their partners, their offspring and sometimes for others as well. Of course we cannot ever prove that cats, dogs, elephants, porpoises or chimpanzees possess consciousness. Maybe their behaviour consists of no more than instinctive responses to appropriate stimuli. But the same can be said about other human beings. How do I know that they possess consciousness? Of course they can employ the term *consciousness* and assure me that they have it, but how do I know that they really do possess it? In the end we can say no more than that if we have consciousness ourselves, we will be disposed to believe that entities that resemble us also have it. But how much something else resembles us is a matter of degree. Other human beings resemble us greatly in terms of their physical composition, their biological needs and their behaviour. So if I see someone who screams as he immerses his hand in boiling water, I am ready to believe that he is experiencing pain. Sophisticated computer-controlled robots resemble us in some of the things they do, which may even include 'speaking', but the differences seem so important that we are not disposed to think of them as conscious. A computer might emit a high-pitched noise if a sensor comes into contact with boiling water, but if I think of the source of the sound as a computer, I will not suppose that it is really a scream, because I do not think that a computer can be in pain.

The 'higher' non-human animals are unlike us in some ways, but resemble us in others. If a chimpanzee puts an arm in boiling water and emits a piercing noise, I am disposed to think that it is screaming in pain. To the extent that some of our needs are similar to those of other animals, there seems little reason to suppose that those needs which are not shared must be seen as more important. If for example we became convinced that chimpanzees need affection if they are to thrive, would we think that this demonstrated that the need for affection was any less important an ingredient of the good life for human beings than we had previously supposed?

The second point is that not every exercise of our distinctively human capacities is something on which there will be general agreement that we should pride ourselves. Only human beings have the possibility of being blackmailers or of fire-bombing their enemies. Of course it can be argued that we cannot be language-users or acquire mastery of technology without also having the potential for using these capacities for ill. No doubt we ought to aspire to a life in which our potentialities, including those which are distinctively human, are exercised in cooperation rather than conflict with others. But why should it be thought that we act more in accordance with our nature as human beings when we cooperate with others than when we fight them or seek to dominate them? If we have difficulty embracing some of the assumptions that are entailed by the foundational belief that the good life consists in the realization of those capacities which are characteristically and distinctively human, we might try to reformulate the foundational belief. We might suggest that the truly foundational belief of the Marxist is in the intrinsic desirability of life within a community of economic equals. This gives rise to issues which I shall later explore in the context of constitutional socialism.

There is one other ethical feature of Marx's case to which I wish to give a preliminary mention. This concerns his view of political morality. I have already claimed that although Marx had no interest in moral argument as such, he does implicitly advance moral opinions of his own. In particular he believes that the transition to socialism would represent a liberation of the human spirit and that this constitutes a reason for seeking to bring about such a change. Naturally revolutionary activity will be contrary to the prevalent morality within capitalist society, but Marx regards such morality as no more than a cover for bourgeois economic interests and therefore not to be taken seriously. If, as I suggest, one may legitimately represent Marx as having moral opinions, we may say that for Marx the moral priority is to adopt the means that are most likely to promote and perpetuate the socialist revolution. In other words everything should be subordinated to the political struggle. The significance of this view is another question to which I shall return.

14

A Constitutional Alternative?

To desire equality is not . . . to cherish the romantic illusion
that men are equal in character and intelligence. It is to hold
that, while their natural endowments differ profoundly, it is
the mark of a civilised society to aim at eliminating such
inequalities as have their source, not in individual differences,
but in its own organisation; and that individual differences,
which are a source of social energy, are more likely to
ripen and find expression if social inequalities are, as far as
practical, diminished.

R. H. Tawney, *Equality*

Although Marx is undoubtedly the most systematic of all socialist
writers and the one whose writings have attracted the largest
number of followers, the majority of those in the West who regard
themselves as socialists do not view themselves as Marxists. Most
of the successful parties of the left in the Western World, although
they have included Marxist elements, have not been officially
committed to Marxism. Here I refer to parties which have been
members of the Socialist International, and whose members frequently characterize themselves as 'democratic socialists'. Charac-
terizing them as constitutional socialists helps us to navigate
around disputes about different conceptions of democracy (see
chapter 2) and also brings out the fact that these parties are in
general sympathetic to the ideas enshrined in the constitutions of
Western states. Support for these ideas is not of course confined
to Westerners. In most Western countries parties belonging to the
Socialist International have spent many years in government but

in recent times have mostly been in retreat. Some, like the British Labour Party and the Federal German SPD, have suffered a series of electoral defeats and were in opposition throughout all or almost all of the 1980s. Others, like the Australian Labor Party, the New Zealand Labour Party and the French Socialist Party, retained office during most of this period but on the basis of such pragmatic policies that it is not easy to say what is distinctively socialist about the governments that they formed. Only in Scandinavia were there socialist parties which arguably retained their distinctive character and combined this with electoral success. In considering the ideas of constitutional socialism, I shall therefore be looking not so much at the policy ideas of recent 'left-wing' governments, but at the ideas associated in the past with intellectuals and intellectually minded politicians, such as Beatrice and Sidney Webb, R. H. Tawney, Aneurin Bevan and Antony Crosland.

Sidney Webb wrote about the nature of change in the following terms:

> Important organic changes will necessarily be (1) democratic, and thus acceptable to a majority of the people and prepared for in the minds of all; (2) gradual, and thus causing no dislocation, however rapid may be the rate of progress; (3) not regarded as immoral by the mass of people, and thus not subjectively demoralising to them; and in this country, at any rate; (4) constitutional and peaceful.[1]

This concern with procedural constraints might lead us to wonder whether the difference between Marxists and constitutional socialists is a difference about means rather than ends. So far as ultimate ends are concerned, it is difficult to be clear about the extent of agreement amongst socialists, whether Marxist or not, since the nature of socialism is usually spelled out in negatives, for example that socialism means a classless society, or in generalities, such as those of the Gotha Programme, or in vaguely defined ideals such as the commitment to equality or fraternity or human dignity. I am not suggesting that these are empty phrases incapable of being fleshed out in more positive or more specific terms. Indeed I shall have something to say about attempts to do this. But since socialist writers and politicians operating in a capitalist society do not feel the need to devote much time or energy to the exposition of the precise details of the ends to which they are committed, it is hard to quantify the extent to which the ultimate goal is one that commands general agreement amongst them. It would help of course if there were some generally accepted historical examples of socialist societies, but there are not. So the extent to which Marxists and other socialists disagree about ends must remain a matter of dispute. It is possible however to say something about the different attitudes of Marxists and constitutional socialists to the way in which their ideal is to be realized.

Sometimes it is assumed, particularly perhaps by those who regard socialism as a threat, that constitutional socialism is characterized simply by the belief that there is a parliamentary route to communism. This belief differs from Marx's own position in holding that in certain unusual historical circumstances the legal and constitutional mechanisms that have evolved in order to defend the interests of the capitalist class can be turned effectively in the opposite direction and used to destroy capitalism. This is no more than a tactical development of Marx's thinking and indeed has represented the view of many in the Communist Parties of Western Europe. There is no fundamental conflict here with Marx's view that the state evolves in order to buttress the interest of the dominant class, since history furnishes a number of examples of constitutional provisions which, like those of the Weimar Republic, have produced opposite effects to those intended.

However Marxists who support Western constitutions do so for tactical reasons. They may believe it unwise or imprudent or impossible to seek to move without electoral support from capitalism to socialism, but their reason for endorsing Western-style elections is not that they believe that the establishment of a socialist society would otherwise be illegitimate. Their position is in effect that of our hypothetical Polish communist (see chapter 7) in relation to the right to worship.

Constitutional socialists may however see Western-type democracy not just as an instrument for making the transition to socialism but as an expression of the *right* of citizens not to be governed without their consent. We observed in chapter 7 that rights are a characteristically liberal concept. Like many liberal values they serve to restrict what may properly be done as part of the political struggle. For Marxists such values have become emphasized in liberal societies precisely in order to protect the interests of the class that has power. However in endorsing the rights of representative democracy, constitutional socialists indicate that they are in the business of trying to reconcile traditional liberal values with a commitment to progressing to a society regulated by the egalitarian principle of the Gotha Programme. But for constitutional socialists, political morality operates within the framework of liberal values. Might not such a framework prove an obstacle to the achievement of significant progress towards economic equality?

The Importance of Economic Growth

Now to give a reasonably high priority to economic growth is not . . . to accept a Tory philosophy – rather, indeed, the reverse . . . And it is certainly also a pre-condition of attaining office.
Antony Crosland, The Future of Socialism

Seeking to achieve a marriage of economic equality with traditional liberal values gives rise to a practical problem. If the transition to socialism must be acceptable to public opinion, then in a capitalist society oriented towards material consumption, a socialist party cannot readily make challenges to the existing standard of living of too many of the public. That is why the British Labour Party has for many years been confronted with the problem of reconciling its commitment to greater economic equality with its desire to reassure voters that it is committed neither to spectacular increases in taxation nor to a wholesale assault on private property. Socialists have not been unaware of the need to resolve this dilemma, and socialist politicians have constantly been at pains to reassure voters that they propose to increase taxation only for the wealthiest and do not threaten the property of the ordinary citizen.

Thus Hugh Gaitskell, leader of the British Labour Party, made a famous pledge two weeks before the 1959 General Election that 'there will be no increase in the standard or other rates of income tax so long as normal peacetime conditions continue'[2] and Aneurin Bevan, the inspiration of the Left in the post-war British Labour Party, claimed that socialism struggles 'against the evils that flow from private property, yet realizes that all forms of private property are not necessarily evil'.[3]

Offering reassurances to all but the wealthiest is all very well, but since the wealthiest are small as a proportion of the total population in a capitalist society, the amount of increased revenue that can be generated in this way is limited. Mr Denis Healey, who shortly before he became Chancellor of the Exchequer had declared that there would be 'howls of anguish from the eighty thousand people who are rich enough to pay over seventy-five per cent on the last slice of their income'[4] was subsequently to conclude that 'any substantial attempt to improve the lot of the poorest section of the population must now be at the expense of the average man and woman, since the very rich do not collectively earn enough to make much difference, and the average man does not nowadays want to punish those who earn a little more than he, since he hopes ultimately to join them'.[5]

Something else is needed to solve the problem and for many years it was found in Crosland's commitment to growth. For many years the commitment to growth featured in the election platforms of socialist parties. Thus the British Labour Party Manifesto in 1959 declared that 'Tory propagandists allege that a Labour Government would have to put up taxes in order to pay for these improved social services. This is quite untrue. The finance required would be raised in two ways. The chief way . . . will be though planned expansion.'[6] Nearly three decades later, the New Zealand Labour Party was promising in its 1987 Policy Document that 'Labour will overcome the legacy of the past and make continued progress toward sustainable economic growth' and the Australian Labor Party was promising voters that it would 'give priority to economic recovery, a fair distribution of the benefits of economic growth and improvements in the welfare and standard of living of the Australian people'.[7]

Clearly if the interventionist economic policies favoured by socialists could painlessly generate economic growth, then this would provide the means of bringing about greater economic equality, without damaging the existing standard of living of too many of those whose support is needed by a socialist government. In these circumstances it would be possible to reconcile the commitment to the values of liberal democracy with the pursuit of greater economic equality. But this means that constitutional socialists have to make certain demands of the facts. Unless it is the case that socialist governments have a greater capacity to generate a significant degree of economic growth, they will be forced either to make an assault on the economic position of those who are comfortably off or to fail to make any real progress towards equality.

This is more than a theoretical dilemma for socialists. It has been a rock on which socialist governments have foundered time and time again. Aneurin Bevan used to speak of taking over the 'commanding heights of the economy' in order to realize the aim spelled out in Clause 4 of the Party constitution. This compound aim is

> to secure for the workers by hand or by brain the full fruits of their industry and the most equitable distribution thereof that may be possible upon the basis of the common ownership of the means of production, distribution and exchange, and the best obtainable system of popular administration and control of each industry or service.

But how can such an aim ever be achieved in a modern industrial democracy? In the years after the Second World War, socialists in Britain thought that the solution lay in taking industries into public ownership. At that time it proved possible for the state to take over industries like coal, steel and the railways. However as a result of the effects of war the industries were not in a profitable condition and the former owners were content to accept compensation.

But how can profitable industry ever be taken over? The problem is that those who occupy favoured economic positions are well-placed to defend themselves against constitutional attempts to implement socialism in one country. In the modern world where investment knows no national boundaries, disinvestment and economic crisis are likely to precede the passage of any legislation designed to implement the socialist programme. Although socialist governments might ban the export of capital, much of the capital is likely to have departed well before a government committed to such a programme has held its first Cabinet meeting. Similar considerations also apply to attempts at substantial redistribution through the taxation system, or attempts to control profits. Those who have the economic power are always in a position to pass on increased taxation costs to others, either in the form of higher prices or lower real wages. If it seems to them that this will not work, they still have the option of transferring their investments elsewhere.

So the stimulation of growth is essential for constitutional socialists. Unfortunately this aim is itself problematic. In fact the two most recent of the manifesto statements quoted above are distinctly more cautious than the first. The Australian statement refers to the distribution of the benefits of growth but leaves open the degree of importance of actually achieving it. The New Zealand statement is clear in the commitment to growth, but couples it with the requirement that the growth must be 'sustainable'. The difficulty has arisen from the realization that the measures which encourage growth, such as low interest rates and a policy of public investment, also stimulate inflation and diminish market confidence. So exactly the same strategic reasons that lead constitutional socialist politicians to offer reassurances that they will not significantly increase tax burdens for the majority also provide a reason for caution in adopting a commitment to growth. In 1990 Mr John Smith, the British Labour Party's spokesman on economic affairs, was telling the American business community that 'there will be no dash for growth under the next Labour Government'.[8] But the problem is not confined to the issue of whether socialist governments are likely to be effective in promoting growth in a sustainable and measured way without triggering an economic crisis.

The other difficulty concerns the question of whether further economic growth in already developed parts of the world can be endorsed by socialists as a good thing. The underlying issue concerns the appropriate attitude for socialist governments to adopt to the interests of the citizens of other and especially of poorer countries. Presumably commitments to equality and human dignity are not supposed to come to a halt at national frontiers. Is it not the case that the pursuit of ever-increasing standards of living in the Western world is damaging to the third world? Even if it can be argued that ever increasing prosperity in the West creates a larger market for the goods produced by poor countries, there seems reason to fear the global environmental consequences triggered by the increased demand for energy which accompanies greater prosperity. So it looks as if the only environmentally safe way in which third world poverty could ever be alleviated would have to involve a significant transfer of wealth from Western countries to poorer countries. Since socialists characteristically voice a concern for all humanity, should we not then expect them to advocate a reduction rather than an increase in the prevalent standards of living in the West?

The practical problem for socialists committed to operating within the constraints of Western constitutions is that no government which is dependent on winning elections can be seen to be indifferent between the economic well-being of its own citizens and the similar well-being of others. The underlying theoretical question is whether it is possible to reconcile an equal concern for all humanity with the view that a government has a duty to promote the well-being of its own citizens.

This latter question touches on a philosophical debate about *general* and *special* moral claims. This distinction was initially drawn in respect of rights.[9] Special rights are ones which people have as a result either of past transactions between individuals or of personal relationships. General rights are the moral rights that all people have, and are thus independent of all relationships or transactions. So my friend's right to the return of a book that I had borrowed would count as a special right, whereas his right not to be assaulted would count as a general right. Equally we could say that my duty to return the book is a special duty, whereas the duty of everyone not to assault my friend, is a general duty.

Should socialists concede that governments have a special duty to promote the interests of their citizens, even where this might be damaging to the interests of others? The reality is that the world is structured in such a way that any government must have special duties in respect of its own subjects. If for example we thought that the government of the United States should show equal and impartial concern for the welfare of all mankind and have no special concern for its own citizens, then in order to secure this result we might advocate that everyone should be allowed to vote in American elections or indeed to run for Congress or the Presidency. Clearly in these circumstances the United States would have ceased to be a sovereign state. To suppose that governments do not have special duties to their own citizens would be like imagining that there could be families within which there were no special obligations. Parents do not imagine that when giving presents they should be impartial between their own and their neighbour's children. It does not ordinarily seem relevant to object to my giving presents to my children on the ground that other people's children may have greater needs.

It is clear then that existing social structures and personal relationships make a moral difference to how we ought to behave. It may therefore be reasonable, as David Miller has argued, for socialists to focus on communities that actually exist.[10] But what those who are seriously committed to any non-trivial conception of economic equality as a long-term goal cannot do is to favour the pursuit of the economic well-being of some people in circumstances in which this prevents others from being able similarly to secure their own well-being. At least my giving presents to my children does not preclude other parents from giving presents to their children. But the worry of environmentalists is that our planet's reserves of fossil fuels are being depleted as a direct result of the life-styles of those who inhabit the developed world. In other words the way in which Western governments pursue the economic well-being of their own citizens may make it impossible for third world citizens to attain a much more modest standard of living. Even if the pessimists who believe that we have already damaged our environment beyond repair are wrong, few believe that the planet can indefinitely accommodate an average standard of living for all mankind which approximates to that now enjoyed in the West. So although socialist egalitarians may be able to reconcile a theoretical commitment to the desirability of attaining a signicant degree of economic equality for all with the judgement that governments have special obligations to pursue the well-being of their own citizens, they might be expected to add that no government should seek to attain for its own citizens a level of economic well-being which exceeds that which could be universally achieved.

My suggestion is that socialists need to argue in one of three ways. One possibility is that they maintain that fears about the capacity of the planet to sustain high standards of living for all are unjustified. The acceptability of this course will turn on what we make of the factual evidence. The second option is to advocate a significant reduction in the material standard of living enjoyed in the West, which some people would think is not practical politics. The third possibility is that they spell out a conception of economic equality in a way that does not call into question the freedom of people in the developed world to enjoy a higher standard of living than they are ready to permit to others, which may be thought tantamount to a concession that the brotherhood of man is little more than an empty slogan.

Our discussion of the feasibility of constitutional socialism has so far revolved around practical questions. I have sought to show that constitutional socialism resembles Marxism in that it makes certain demands of the facts. To that extent we have been considering questions to which there is the possibility of arriving at rationally justified answers. Purely factual questions are of course relevant to evaluative ones. As I suggested above, there can be no moral requirement to do the impossible. The nature of the connection is captured by the Kantian dictum that 'ought entails can'. The point of this is to assert that any situation that we ought to bring about is one that we must be able to bring about. The converse is that where we cannot do something, it cannot be the case that we ought to do it. Constitutional socialists need to respond to the objection that their egalitarian objectives simply cannot be brought about within the framework of the constitutional commitments which they endorse.

Constitutional Socialism and Economic Equality

Let us suppose that these difficulties are ones that can be satisfactorily solved. Having previously noted the plasticity of the concept of equality (see chapter 2), it is appropriate for us to enquire how socialist egalitarians believe that their commitment to economic equality should be fleshed out. The constitutional socialists' ideal cannot be that each individual should have assets that would be valued equally in the hypothetical market-place of a *laissez-faire* economy, since such values would not be determinable. But in any case the underlying concern of many socialists is typically not with the pursuit of precise economic equality but with the promotion of social equality, to which gross economic inequality is viewed as an obstacle. Tawney put it in the following way.

> What is repulsive is not that one man should earn more than others, for where community of environment, and a common education and habit of life, have bred a common tradition of respect and consideration, these details of the counting-house are forgotten or ignored. It is that some classes should be excluded from the heritage of civilisation . . . and that the fact of human fellowship . . . should be obscured by economic contrasts, which are trivial and superficial.[11]

This passage provides a guide to interpreting Tawney's wish, quoted earlier, to see social inequalities diminished to the extent that this is 'practical'. This concept is unhelpfully fuzzy. Taken in one way we might suppose that the practical is simply what we can reasonably expect to achieve if we try. But then how much equality is practical turns on how single-minded, or to put it another way how *ruthless*, we are. One might observe that Pol Pot succeeded in demonstrating how the most far-reaching schemes might yet be practical. Of course what was practical for Pol Pot would be impractical for socialists committed to proceeding within the constraints of Western constitutions. Such socialists cannot, as Webb recognized, affront the strongly held moral perceptions of the public. In the relevant sense it is not practical for a socialist government to bring in budgetary measures aimed at ensuring equal incomes for all, because many people would find such a policy grossly unreasonable. It is however notorious that people disagree about what is grossly unreasonable or immoral, and that perceptions in such matters may change. So it would clearly be absurd to prescribe the precise limits of what is reasonable not only in present circumstances, but for the foreseeable future.

It is clear however from Tawney's emphasis on the value of individual differences that, whatever might prove to be practical, his objection to Pol Pot would not have been confined to the latter's coercive methods. It is not just that Tawney might object to some equalization proposals on the ground that public opinion could not be persuaded to support them, but that he himself would be fundamentally opposed to a mechanical pursuit of equality, because he desires a society which is not characterized by a 'counting-house' mentality. The problem for Tawney is that there is no clear-cut distinction, along the lines he described, between inequalities that have their source in individual differences and ones that have their source in social organization. Individual differences no doubt are the product of a whole complex of factors, but this complex includes the individual's own perception of the society in which he lives. Thus social changes are always liable, though perhaps sometimes in ways that are not easily predicted or understood, to result in changes in individual interests, aptitudes and personalities. Even differences in the physical well-being of individuals can be affected by social organization. Social scientists tell us that in Britain even such indicators of survival prospects and life chances as birth weight can be correlated with the social class of the mother.[12]

A less intractable question than either the provenance of individual differences or that of what is reasonable concerns who is to determine what is reasonable. A suggested answer to this question is contained in the passage quoted earlier from Clause 4 of the Constitution of the British Labour Party. What this does is to focus on the socialist concern with ownership of the means of production, distribution and exchange. Moreover it insists not that everyone should have equal individual ownership, which could be achieved by providing all citizens with equal shares in industrial enterprises, but that these enterprises should be *commonly* owned and controlled. Similarly it is clear that what Tawney wishes to promote is 'fellowship'. So we can think of the socialist concern with economic equality in terms of the requirement that the most important economic decisions should be taken in accordance with the desires of the people as a whole.

Fraternity and Community

Thus socialist politicians focus on the ownership of coal-mines rather than of hairdressing salons. That they do not specify the precise degree of equality of wealth which they advocate also indicates that they are not fundamentally concerned with the mathematics of the ratio of the wealth enjoyed respectively by the richest and the poorest. Socialist economic objectives, I suggest, are inspired by opposition to those economic relationships in which some people dominate others. Such domination is held to be inevitable in a society in which economic activity is predominantly geared to the attainment of private purposes. Economic inequalities are focused on because they are so far-reaching in their implications for the ability of men and women to lead worthwhile lives. The prescribed remedy is to view the production and distribution as a common or collective enterprise. So socialists are ultimately concerned with the quality of relationships that exist within the community. Their emphasis on economic equality reflects their conviction that economic disadvantage has a pervasive and damaging effect on the life prospects of those who are disadvantaged and also on their ability to see themselves and be seen by others as full members of the community. In terms of a slogan, this is represented sometimes by Tawney's term *fellowship*, but more often as an appeal to *fraternity*. This term is intended to call attention to the bond that is forged between people who participate as equal partners in a shared enterprise. As Crick puts it, fraternity 'is an attitude of mind, and one associated with activity. Fraternity is not radiating an abstract love of humanity: it arises from people actually working together towards common ends.'[13]

We noted earlier that liberals are committed to an individualist conception and conservatives to an organic conception of community. Constitutional socialists, we now have reason to observe, are collectivists rather than individualists. This is because their conception of equality is not that each individual should achieve an equal pay-off for himself, but that all should join together in a partnership for the benefit of all. However the term *organic* is not so well suited to the socialist as to the conservative conception of community, since the model of an organism suggests that some citizens might naturally be expected to play a much more important role than others, just as the functioning of the liver is more important than that of the larynx. The point about fraternity is that the partnership is seen as one of equals.

To understand the ideal of fraternity we need to distinguish between shared aims and collective ones. The pursuit of individual self-interest often brings us into conflict, but sometimes leads us into cooperation. Thus if two people who have no concern for each other both want to go to an island, the only available means of transport is a large rowing boat, and the distance is too far for either of them to row by himself, they will have to share the work of rowing. These people at least initially have a shared aim but not a collective one. It just so happens that neither can do anything to get himself to the island that will not also serve to get the other there. Similarly my neighbours and I might be anxious that the water supply to our houses is being polluted. Each of us may be concerned just for our own water, and have no concern for the purity of anyone else's supply. We have no collective aim but we do have a shared one.

We can contrast such cases with others, which can readily develop out of the sharing of aims, in which our concern is not only for ourselves but also for those who share our aims. Suppose in the first example that one of the oarsmen explains that his visit to the island is to try to find a friend with whom he has lost touch. It is possible that the hearer will find his sympathies engaged so that he ends up by caring about whether his companion succeeds. Or imagine in the second case that my neighbours and I have campaigned for years to secure a purer water supply and the campaign succeeds just as I am about to move out of the area. Is my primary feeling one of regret that I wasted so much time in a campaign that has proved of no benefit to me, or of satisfaction that my neighbours will now enjoy cleaner water? The latter would be an indication that I had come to view the aim as a collective one.

For present purposes let us accept the empirical claim that the spirit of fellowship and fraternity with fellow citizens develops most readily in a community whose economic life is organized in such a way that all of the members are encouraged to regard themselves as equal partners. There is still a question as to whether there is any good reason for endorsing this ideal. One might note a parallel between the constitutional socialist's emphasis on fraternity and the Marxist view that human beings fulfil themselves when they act in cooperation with one another. In relation to the latter view, we observed that human beings had the potential for both cooperation and conflict but left open the question of why the former should be thought more authentically human. In the case of the ideal of fraternity, we may observe that people do sometimes experience fraternal feelings, particularly perhaps in circumstances where they are subject to a common danger, but wonder why it is thought necessary that it should play such an important part in the good life.

An answer to these questions may be found in the way in which socialists conceive the relationship between the individual and the community. Earlier we noted that Marx referred to his conception of human nature as man's 'species-being'. An implication of the use of what is at any rate to English-speaking readers an unfamiliar noun is that Marx was interested not so much in the good life for a man or woman but in the good life for mankind. This collectivist presumption is important in that once we have made it, we will find it plausible to suppose that our potentiality for cooperation and fellowship is a more faithful expression of human nature than our potentiality for competitiveness and conflict. Whilst it may be possible to argue that the good life for an individual can be realized through the exercise of power and dominion over others, such a conception of the good life is one that cannot be enjoyed by everyone. So the good life for mankind cannot be a life of domination.

A similar point can be made about the attractions of fraternity. It is easy to make the assumption that men and women should view themselves as brothers and sisters, once we are convinced that the most important objectives are common ones. Perhaps it is no accident that a spirit of unity and fellowship most readily arises in the face of common enemy or danger. In circumstances of battle, soldiers may, without a second thought, perform acts of the most extreme heroism in order to protect their comrades. Plainly if there is a war to be won, it is an enormous advantage to have soldiers who will unhesitatingly give priority to the common cause rather to their own survival or to furthering their military careers.

But what good reason is there to assume that the most important ends are not the ends of the individual rather than those of the community or of mankind? The spirit of fraternity, which leads us to take great pride and satisfaction in our common achievements, may seem intrusive and restrictive if we are committed to individual goals. The extreme communitarian will of course claim that there are no legitimate goals which are purely individual. So those who wish to spend their time reading or writing poetry or novels or philosophy or in such pursuits as gardening, ornithology or hill-walking would have to be seen as anti-social, unless these were activities which the community itself could view as being in the interests of the people as a whole. An individual's desire to do his own thing would always be everyone else's business.

I remarked in chapter 7 that extreme individualism was a position advanced by few if any, but that it is useful as a reference point because it helps us to understand more moderate individualist positions. A corresponding point may be made about extreme communitarianism. From Marx's almost romantic description, which I quoted earlier, of the freedom to be able spend one's time as hunter, fisherman, shepherd and critic, one may surmise that his ultimate vision of the good life is not one in which every last individual action is subject to the approval of the community as a whole. On the other hand he also thinks that this freedom can only be realized when production is appropriately regulated. Until socialism can be achieved, the Marxist's overriding commitment has, as we have seen, to be to the promotion of these conditions. So where there is any question of conflict between the pursuit of social and individual ends, it is the former which takes priority. Individual freedom is something which can be afforded once the economy is structured along socialist lines. This is totalitarian in the same way as Aristotle's definition of politics (see chapter 3) in that it views all human activity as something which in principle may be regulated in the common interest.

Constitutional socialists are further removed than Marx from extreme communitarianism. Their commitment to the principles of Western constitutions, which seek to define and protect many individual rights, means that they at all times accept the legitimacy of the pursuit of some private objectives. This is still faithful to the fraternal metaphor in that it would hardly be thought to be a feature of the ideal fraternal relationship that someone should be expected to gain the approval of his brothers for everything he does. But the idea of fraternity also suggests a community in which a citizen who is in trouble can confidently look to fellow citizens for spontaneous and uncomplaining help, even perhaps in circumstances where his need may be the result of his own foolishness. Brothers may squabble but, if the bonds are secure, it may be supposed that they will unite in a crisis. In such circumstances what they display is what is described in socialist rhetoric as *solidarity*.

The emphasis on solidarity as a political virtue is a clear indication that constitutional socialism incorporates a significant communitarian element. The greater the importance we attach to the fulfilment of needs, independently of whose needs they are and of how they have arisen, the more we will value a spirit of solidarity since this will enable actions to be geared to the satisfaction of these needs. On the other hand the greater the value we place on the freedom of individuals to make what they will of their lives, provided they respect the similar freedom of others, the more wary we may be about the benefits of solidarity. Consider a community which provides resources to alleviate child poverty.

Solidarity and fraternity may mean that those who are comparatively affluent do not begrudge paying tax for this purpose, because although the poor children are not their children they see the problem as one for the whole community. But it may also mean that a couple who are not confident of their ability to meet the cost of bringing up a child out of their own resources will feel that they have to consider the interests of the whole community before deciding to have children. For some this would be an oppressive denial of individuality.

Is there any way in which we can rationally and definitively resolve the issue of whether individual ends are more or less important than collective ends? I suggest that this question must be answered in the negative. It is an aspect of the human condition that each person has purely individual needs. A mother may suffer if her daughter has toothache. She may even prefer to have the toothache herself. But what she suffers is not toothache. The toothache is the daughter's and cannot be shared even with those closest to her, let alone with the community. Nor is there any feasible set of social arrangements which can make any difference to facts like this. Human beings will always be subject to unhappiness, depression and grief as a result of things going wrong in their lives. Conversely they will experience satisfaction, elation and happiness at their own success. Those without any special concern for self simply would not survive. However it is also an aspect of the human condition that we cannot survive simply as solitary creatures. For most people an important determinant of whether they are happy or depressed is whether things go well or badly to other people with whom they have ties of love and friendship. That young human beings are born helpless and cannot keep themselves alive until many years have passed, that our ability to acquire language presupposes living in a community whose members constantly wish to communicate with each other, and that even the successful businessman motivates his workers to think of themselves as part of a team are all indicative of the fact that our needs are not purely individual. How we rank these individual and shared dimensions of our existence says something about the kind of beings that *we* are. But, as we have already observed, rational argument has to begin somewhere. Put another way, rational argument is about what it is appropriate for *us* to believe. But our needs are different in different places and times. In some communities the abilities to catch fish, to hunt, to make war, to enjoy poetry, to be computer-literate, to make friends easily, or to devote one's time to politics will be more important than in others. There can thus be no argument that is independent of the particularities of time and place for supposing that there is just one way of looking at these matters which is in all circumstances superior to all others.

Further Reading

Most of the books on socialist theory take Marxism as their principal focus. However, for a discussion of the differences between different forms of socialism, see A. Wright, *Socialisms* (Oxford University Press, 1987). For an attempt to reconcile general support for Marxism with philosophical concerns about methodology, see G. A. Cohen, *Karl Marx's Theory of History* (Oxford University Press, 1978). S. Lukes, *Marxism and Morality* (Oxford University Press, 1985) explores the paradox of Marx's attitude to morality and A. Buchanan, *Marx and Justice* (London: Methuen, 1983) contrasts Marxism with Rawlsian liberalism. T. Campbell, *The Left and Rights* (London: Routledge & Kegan Paul, 1983) argues that socialists should not jettison the concept of rights. R. Norman, *Free and Equal* (Oxford University Press, 1987) seeks to rebut criticisms that a socialist conception of equality must be incompatible with freedom. A discussion of general and special obligations can be found in J. S. Fishkin, *The Limits of Obligation*, (New Haven: Yale University Press, 1982).

Part V
Conclusion

15

Where Rational Argument Ends

Before embarking on a discussion of liberalism, conservatism and socialism, I drew attention to the possibility, which I characterized as gloomy, that we might be forced to the conclusion that subjectivism was true and that political beliefs might not be capable of rational vindication. Now is the time to consider whether we can reach a verdict on whether this is so. In the case of all of the different versions of liberalism, conservatism and socialism that we considered, we saw that there was the possibility of raising rational arguments which are relevant to their acceptability.

Clearest of all however is the possibility of rationally demonstrating the *failure* of particular arguments. We saw for example that political arguments fail if they make demands of the facts which are not vindicated by the evidence, and we saw that such charges can be brought against some arguments for welfare liberalism and different forms of socialism. We saw that Marxism can be charged with having a methodology which generates unfalsifiable factual claims which are then taken to have been scientifically established. We saw that an argument for discrimination in employment might fail because the facts to which it appealed were not relevant. We saw that an argument of economic liberals for the legitimacy of the market might be held to fail because it may be accused of confusing the way people behave when subject to a particular kind of political regulation with the way in which they might naturally behave when unregulated. We saw that in attempting to defend themselves against the charge of inconsistency, constitutional socialists might leave themselves vulnerable to the charge of impracticability in committing themselves to a goal that cannot be attained by methods they are willing to accept. We saw that one argument for conservatism might be thought to be of a kind that can be commended only to some people and to depend on the assumption that others will not accept it. That these alleged faults matter is conceded by the fact that defenders of the positions under attack respond to the criticisms with counter-arguments, some of which we may regard as effective defences against particular objections. So as well as the possibility of decis-ive objections against particular arguments, there is also the possi-bility of defusing an objection with an effective counter-attack. But even though our political positions differ from subjective preferences in that we see them as something which we need to defend against objections, nothing we have said indicates any way in which the truth of any of the positions can be convincingly demonstrated. So it is clear that there are pitfalls which rational political arguments must avoid. However in order to arrive at a desired conclusion we have to do more than avoid pitfalls. It is perfectly possible that two or more approaches to politics might avoid all of the pitfalls but still be incompatible with one another. Can we expect ever to find decisive rational arguments *for* a given position?

A mere failure to find such arguments leaves open the logical possibility that they exist but we have simply not been looking in the right places. A longer version of this book might have explored more communitarian versions of liberalism, Trotskyite socialism, and other political ideologies such as nationalism, fas-cism, feminism, environmentalism and various brands of religious fundamentalism. In all cases I would have sought to identify assumptions which adherents take for granted, but which can be readily contested by those who do not embrace the ideology. Are we to suppose that cogent arguments for political beliefs can never be advanced and that all alleged political truths must be fundamentally contestable? Although we sometimes talk about universality, as for example in the context of the human rights which are specified in the United Nations Declaration and which are described as 'universal', is the reality that there is no such thing as universal political truth?

In the course of this book I have on several occasions suggested analogies between political and scientific argument. There is no doubt that the conclusions of scientists, unlike the prescriptions of political thinkers, can often be urged on all mankind. To say this is not to dissent from Popper's view that we cannot prove the truth of physical laws, but only disprove conjectures. But it is to assert that it is for example rational to believe in the universality of gravitational attraction. For although this cannot be proven, the conjecture that the heavy objects of everyday experience, if unsupported, fall towards the centre of the earth has so frequently been exposed to the possibility of disproof and has always come through unscathed that we are unable to form expectations about the future, and unable to do any kind of physics, unless we believe it. This belief may be provisional, in the sense that we are always aware that new facts could in principle be unearthed that would lead us to revise it, but it is a confident not a tentative belief. What makes it so is our high degree of certainty that the cirumstances in which we would revise it will never be encountered.

The rational demonstration of scientific truth is thus relative to our confident assumption that the lessons of experience are not a radically misleading guide to the future. We cannot prove the truth of this assumption for, as we saw in chapter 13, no amount of evidence about what has happened in the past can provide an infallible basis for expectations about what will happen next. To have such expectations is however no more unreasonable than to believe that if we see someone draw the Ace of Spades apparently at random from a complete pack of cards ten times in succession, or a chimpanzee apparently copy-typing *Macbeth*, there is trickery afoot. Moreover it is impossible to see how we can manage to live our lives without making some unprovable assumptions. If we wish to understand the way our world works and to survive in it, we simply have to make assumptions about the future which reflect our experience of the past. We do not have the luxury of being able to wait for cast-iron certainty about what will happen next before we perform our own actions.

So scientific beliefs can be rationally demonstrated, but that demonstration is always relative to particular unprovable assumptions. Does the same hold for political beliefs? We may have found no independent yardstick against which we can measure the merits of individualist or communitarian assumptions, but we have seen how traditional liberal arguments presuppose individualist assumptions and in different ways traditional conservative and socialist arguments presuppose communitarian or collectivist ones. The difference between the cases of science and politics is that in the latter case the option of declining to make the particular assumptions that are urged on us always seems open. But if we accept that there are no foundational political principles which must be endorsed by all, the question arises as to the basis of our own political opinions. If we know that our principles rest on disputable assumptions, are our political beliefs not built on shifting sands? How can we recognize an assumption as disputable without demonstrable error and still make it? If we do not think that any set of principles can be shown to be superior to its competitors, this may lead us to wonder how we can ever come to regard any principles as *ours*. Must we then despair?

16

Principles and Foundations

It is a mistake to suppose that our political principles constitute a foundation in the sense of a platform upon which are erected our opinions on all detailed policy issues. The relationship between principles and our actions and opinions is altogether more subtle than this foundationalist picture suggests. The reason is that although principles sometimes function as moral generalizations which we can invoke to justify particular actions, on other occasions we amend our principles because we cannot accept the actions that the principles demand.

This can be illustrated by reference to the way in which we come to adopt and adapt our personal morality. Suppose that I have hitherto subscribed to the principle that one ought never to tell lies. Now however a friend has given me some information about his intention to apply for a particular post and I have agreed to keep this secret. I am then asked by someone else whether my friend will apply for the post. My options here are to lie, to tell the truth, or not to answer the question. The principle of never telling lies would lead me to choose between telling the truth and not answering the question. I may reject the option of telling the truth since this will be a clear breach of my friend's confidence. The option of not answering may therefore seem best, and perhaps will be best if I can be sure that my evasion of the question or refusal to answer does not provide a clear indication of what my friend told me. There will however be occasions in which failure to answer will signal my friend's intentions as unmistakably as would the truthful answer. In these circumstances I may feel that it too would constitute a betrayal of his trust. Further reflection might lead me to suppose that if I am not prepared to betray my friend's secret and I wish to remain absolutely faithful to the principle of never telling lies, I should in future never accept a friend's confidence or perhaps I should make a habit of never answering questions about what I know of other people's intentions, because if this is perceived by others to be my consistent practice, my failure to answer on a given occasion will not lead my hearers to accurate conclusions about what I have been told in confidence. Yet I may also conclude that it would be absurd to go through life never permitting my friends to trust to my discretion or never answering innocent questions so that I can get away with a refusal to answer when I really need to. Maybe, I might conclude, I should permit a small amendment to the principle of never telling lies. Perhaps I even consider the morally fraught course of finding a definition of lying which will allow me to give a false answer and still maintain that I have not told a lie. This latter option does of course still involve a change of principle, but it allows me to conceal from others and perhaps from myself that this is what I have done.

What applies to personal morality also holds for politics. Suppose that I hold the belief that the problem of Ireland should be solved in accordance with the principle of self-determination. This principle holds that all peoples have a right to govern themselves, and leads me to assert that there should be an all-Ireland plebiscite to resolve the question of Irish unity. But then it is pointed out to me that given the Unionist majority in Northern Ireland, it is clear that the right of the people of Ireland to self-determination would in practice be incompatible with the right of the people of Northern Ireland to govern themselves. In these circumstances I either have to abandon my belief in the principle of self-determination, or opt to find a definition of 'people' which may be satisfied by one group or the other, but not both.

This alternative picture of the relationship between principles and practice, which Rawls characterized as *reflective equilibrium*,[1] allows our principles to be tested against experience. It is still the case that practice can be underpinned by principle, because there remain many occasions on which I appeal to my amended principle not to tell lies, and on which I can support self-determination. But what happens when I find that my principle indicates that I should carry out an action or support a policy about which I am uneasy is that I must choose either to amend my principle or to act in accordance with it despite my unease. This choice is not one that I can simply make according to whim. Any principle I accept must fit coherently with my other principles. It must be one which I believe can be consistently applied and I have to believe that I shall be content for it to be so applied. I cannot cavalierly change my existing principles whenever their retention would prove inconvenient, because generalizations to which I have no intention of adhering in hard times simply cannot count as my principles, but I must be prepared to modify them in the light of new information or of situations that I have previously neither encountered nor anticipated. This non-foundationalist view of principles was implicit in chapter 13. There I argued that Marx's belief that the good life consists in the exercise of those of our capacities which are characteristically and distinctively human would need to be revised if we made different assumptions about non-human animals.

Although we may be led to formulate our principles in a way that matches our convictions on particular issues, this does not mean that the relationship between principle and practice is symmetrical. From the fact that I support a given policy which is an implementation of a particular principle, it does not follow that I support the principle. I may be against censoring a declaration of support for a terrorist organization, not because I support the principle of freedom of speech but because I judge that the attempt at censorship will probably be counter-productive. The more one knows about which policies are supported and which opposed by a given individual the easier it is to make a conjecture about his underlying principles, particularly given the assumption of ideological connectedness. But as a matter of logic, no matter how well-informed I am about the views of that individual on particular policy issues, I can never deduce that he must subscribe to some given political principle.

If principles are not logically derived from policy beliefs, how can it be that our views on policy may lead us to reconsider our principles? To understand this we need to grasp how selecting a principle differs from a task which can be definitively solved such as completing a jigsaw puzzle. Let us first of all consider a scientific principle such as the conservation of energy. In effect this principle directs the physicist as to the possibilities to which she should be alert. So if a rubber ball is dropped from a height of 5 metres on to a flat concrete surface and rebounds to a height of 3 metres, the physicist will be guided to find the 'lost' energy in the sound of the impact and in an increase in the temperature of both ball and concrete, and will thus be enabled to make better sense of the world. The more accurate the predictions we are able to make about the future, the better are our chances of making sense of the world we inhabit.

It is however important to realize that the fact that we may be able to make accurate predictions does not of itself demonstrate that we can make sense of the world. For example the ebb and flow of the tides could be predicted with a high degree of accuracy on the basis of observation, even if it did not occur to us that the phenomenon was a consequence of the gravitational effect of the moon. We cannot however believe that we are able to make sense of what occurs until we also have a theory within which the phenomenon seems to fit.

The question of whether we have made the best possible sense of the world is different in kind from that of whether a jigsaw puzzle has been solved. In the latter case, the task is to rearrange the pieces to precisely the same relative positions they occupied when the puzzle was cut. So there is one definitively correct solution. But making sense of our experience of the world is more like the exercise of rearranging the letters in the words of this sentence so as to make the funniest possible joke. Even if some inventive person who is confronted with this formidable task succeeds in making a really good joke, we cannot conclude that this is the definitively correct solution to the problem. This would be true even if we could establish that we had found every possible sentence in English which consists of the same letters as the one we are trying to rearrange. The reason is that jokes are never amusing or funny *simpliciter* but only to particular hearers or readers. This is not to say that what is funny or amusing is a purely individual matter. If someone in our society consistently professes to be amused by events or 'jokes' that are found funny by no-one else we ever encounter, we conclude not that he has an eccentric sense of humour but that he is suffering from some kind of mental disturbance or perhaps has no grasp of the concepts involved. When someone finds a joke funny, we do not necessarily expect that he can describe exactly what he finds amusing, for the point of some jokes may be very hard to articulate. But we would certainly expect that he could find some way of communicating the joke to at least some others in his society. We would however neither require nor expect that the point of the jokes we enjoy can be communicated, even with the help of expert translation, to those whose cultural traditions are radically different. Navajo Indians might well tell jokes to one another, but we have no reason to expect that they will be amused by the same jokes that we find funny.

In theory a similar consideration applies in the case of principles intended to enable us to make sense of the universe. Such principles may enable us to make better sense than we can with the help of any alternative principle that occurs to us. But not only must our endorsement of a scientific principle be provisional because we cannot entirely exclude the possibility that future events may surprise us, but even then we must remember that nothing ever makes sense *simpliciter*. It makes sense to particular people with access to particular information and who make particular assumptions. For example doing a rain dance in the hope of ending a drought makes sense to people who assume that the weather is in the gift of gods who need to be propitiated, but makes no sense to meteorologists or Western agriculturalists. There remains a sense however in which scientific principles are more universal than principles of humour. Irrespective of where they live, human beings have very similar requirements for their physical survival. In all parts of the world people are dependent on obtaining food, shelter and warmth. To take an obvious case, we all need water. This factor is so important in parts of the world where it is in short supply that we can expect people to make fairly accurate observations about the incidence of rainfall. The objective superiority of meteorology over rain dancing is attested to by the fact that once rain-dancers become interested enough to seek to understand what contemporary meteorologists tell them, they abandon rain-dancing. Western farmers on the other hand, however avidly they read works of anthropology, do not abandon their craft in favour of rain-dancing.

So what distinguishes the choice of scientific principles is not that it can be achieved without resort to unprovable assumptions. Rather it is that the similarities in physical existence for all man-kind are such that we nearly all end up accepting the same infor-mation as constituting the relevant data, making the same assump-tions and placing confidence in the same predictions based on previously well-tested but unfalsified hypotheses. But whereas we all need the same science, we do not all need the same kind of humour. Whether all men and women need some kind of humour is a question on which I am not qualified to pronounce. But certainly some of us benefit from the possession of a capacity for humour. Plainly however there is no reason to suppose that all human societies are so similar that humour must be the same everywhere and at all times. So humour is certainly culturally-relative in a way that science is not.

When we turn to moral and political principles, our objective is not to make sense of the world but to find a basis that will enable us to share it with others. But we may still ask with which others we are to share the world and in what way? Are we to take seriously the idea that non-human animals should be regarded as partners in this enterprise? Or those yet to be born? Do we need different kinds of principles for cooperating with those who inhabit our own territory than we need for co-existence with foreigners? Can we expect to co-exist with others in the world but not share the resources that are in it?

The importance of these questions is unavoidable, but we delude ourselves if we think we can find some principle which can be applied to find demonstratively correct answers. In chapter 11 I pointed out the inadequacy of any attempt to argue that a utili-tarian principle could prove a secure foundation for conservatism. The point I made there was that conservatism incorporates a commitment to a political culture which, if securely established, will lead to the happiness of those within it, but that it cannot be derived from a principle which is concerned simply with the maximization of happiness. I could of course have made a similar point about any attempt to make a utilitarian case for socialism. No ethical principle which we have arrived at without careful thought about politics can ever provide a neutral basis for a universal resolution of fundamental political questions, because the selection of a principle must reflect the judgement that it provides a good basis for answering the questions. Basic questions about good government are more easily avoided than basic questions of personal morality, but since they are as fundamental we cannot resolve them by neglecting the specifics of the particular issues and concentrating on the application of some abstract general principle.

Plainly the questions posed above are ones which can be answered in different ways. One view is that political morality is a function of our need to reach an accommodation with those who may otherwise damage us. This is the contractualist approach in which we in effect trade our willingness to respect the interests of others for their similar willingness to respect our interests. Such an approach is likely to lead to a liberal rights-centred approach. If we are sympathetic to this kind of thinking we may then have to consider whether and if so how to elaborate it so that it has some application to those individuals who for one reason or another cannot threaten us. So contractualists may differ about how we should view the claims of starving Ethiopians or South Sea islanders threatened by a rise in sea level or future generations or the physically or mentally infirm or foetuses or non-human animals. Also which kind of liberalism it leads to depends on how broadly we conceive of the interests we are concerned to defend. It does not follow from a conviction that we need to reach an agreement with powerful and potentially threatening others that there is a single set of terms that definitively constitutes the agreement which we need to reach.

But we may not wish to adopt the contractualist approach at all. Another possibility is that we think of ourselves not as isolated figures whose interests need to be protected from others, but as possessing an identity which is inextricably bound up with others. If we think in this way, we will be communitarians and will wish to act in ways that reflect this identity. For those who adopt this approach, there are questions about who are the others with whom this identity is shared. There will be questions about how best to maintain that shared identity in a changing world. There will also be questions about the extent to which the citizen's identity also possesses a dimension which is independent of his perception of himself as a member of a community, and the extent to which we are ready to accept that citizens may pursue their individual interests or their group interests within the wider community. There will be questions about the appropriate view to take of interactions with those who are not members of the community.

The questions we have raised are ones to which different answers can be offered. Traditional conservatism and various forms of socialism reflect some of the options. What can be said with confidence is that there is no possibility of demonstrating the definitive correctness of any one set of answers. Take the issue of how we are to identify the community with whose good we are to be concerned. To this question there can be no prescriptive answer. Some communities may be based on affinities of language, some on religion, some on a common history, and some on a shared economic interest. The possibilities are many. What matters in determining whether a group of people constitutes a community is not whether they share one or more of these features but the extent to which *they* think of themselves as members of a community with a shared identity. The importance of affinities of language or religion or history is precisely the importance that the members of the community themselves attach to their shared culture.[2] Nor are perceptions in such matters fixed for all time. So there can be no objectively correct formula which we can apply in an intellectually rigorous way to yield definitive answers as to who constitutes a community. And if this fundamental question is not susceptible to a demonstrably correct answer, it follows that all detailed political questions which presuppose an ability to identify the community are also questions to which we cannot give answers that are justified *without qualification*. This does not mean however that answers cannot be justified within the framework of a given assumption. So we may suppose that within a community whose identity is based on a shared commitment to

Roman Catholicism, there would be general acceptance of the view that abortions should be illegal, for the only opposing arguments would be ones that challenged the basis of the community. But we would look in vain for a conclusive argument which could demonstrate to anyone the correctness or incorrectness of the Catholic view of the moral status of foetuses.

This conclusion may seem to have a relativist flavour but in fact my argument does not entail a general commitment to relativism, if that view is understood as implying that there are no truths which transcend particular cultures. My point is that there are no rationally demonstrable truths except for ones which rest on unprovable assumptions. But relativists in effect hold that what I call unprovable assumptions vary from society to society, whereas I maintain that the circumstances of the human predicament may be such that some of these assumptions transcend cultural differences.

We can now see that the justification of political principles is not structurally different from the justification of scientific principles or for that matter from the justification of the rules of logic or mathematical axioms. Indeed it is because of this structural similarity that a concern with political argument may lead us to a wider interest in philosophy. In all cases the inferences we draw and the conclusions we reach can be justified by reference to certain rules or principles. But these rules or principles are not themselves susceptible to rational justification. To that extent they reflect assumptions but not mere assumptions. They are not mere assumptions because without them we have no basis for understanding our universe or conducting ourselves within it.

17

'Living' and Choosing

The two functions of enabling us to understand the world we inhabit and providing us with a basis for action are rooted in human nature. Though not to a uniform extent, human beings are characterized by intellectual inquisitiveness. Especially is it true of people who read or write books like this that we wish to attain as good an understanding as we can get of the nature of our universe. Moreover it is apparent to each of us that a prime cause of many of the things that go wrong with our lives is to be found in our own actions and those of other people. Indeed some people go so far as to believe that everything that goes wrong, even earthquakes or volcanic eruptions, is a reflection of human wickedness. Though we need not take such extreme views seriously, it is clear that human beings cannot live together or do anything much without some understanding of how far they can trust one another. For example the possibility of my conducting a tutorial in a university only arises because my students and I are confident that we can depend on each other not to attempt to resolve philosophical disagreements with a gun. Moreover we could not do it successfully if we did not think it appropriate to respond to one another's questions. A world in which we make no assumptions is one which we cannot understand and one in which we cannot live.

But what is 'living'? Minimally of course living must involve surviving. So we can certainly dismiss contentions which would result in the speedy demise of those who made them. If ever we encounter someone who claims that there is no good reason for him to believe in the existence of physical objects external to his own person, the appropriate response is not to seek to engage him in argument but to watch how he crosses the road. However I am using the term *living* evaluatively. In this sense to live is not merely to survive but to flourish. Although it would be absurd to seek to lay down a definitive set of conditions as constituting *the* circumstances in which humans will flourish, the range of possibilities is smaller than is sometimes recognized. Whatever cultural differences divide mankind, our biological affinities ensure that there are similarities in our physical needs and our psychological make-up. An impressive illustration of the fact that mankind is not hopelessly divided into different cultural groups with no basis for communication or understanding across the divides is the existence of an international polity. Governments from all parts of the world exchange ambassadors, sign treaties with one another, engage in trade, conduct debates at the United Nations, discuss Human Rights and have shared concerns such as disarmament and the threat posed by environmental hazards. This is not to deny the existence of some people who may have no grasp on concepts such as *government* or *nation-state*, but it is an indication that our world is one in which there are many widely shared concerns.

So the range of assumptions that we might expect to confront is not limitless. Moreover the options for those of us who were brought up and educated in the liberal climate of twentieth century Western culture may be even more restricted. There is an old joke about a lost motorist who stops a passer-by in order to ask for directions to his chosen destination only to be told that he is starting from the wrong place. There is some truth in the suggestion that our human options are limited by where *we* start from. It would be rash to argue that the life of a cannibal or head-hunter is such that human beings who engage in it cannot flourish. But just as people who have once taken meteorology seriously do not become rain-dancers, the life of a head-hunter is not one that *we* can live. The impossibility involved is the impossibility of rejecting the entirety of the past into which one has been socialized. Someone with a background in a Western culture which reflects a Judeo-Christian morality cannot put himself in the position of a primitive head-hunter. Why not? Because primitive head-hunters are not people who have chosen this way of life in the light of an awareness of contemporary Western alternatives.

This claim may be thought by some to be trivial. It might be argued that my claim is true but only by virtue of the fact that no individual can *ever* put himself in exactly the same position as another. Thus so long as A and B are separate individuals, A cannot put himself in B's position in that there must always be some true claims about B's past that cannot be made about A's past. Otherwise A and B would not have separate identities at all. So I cannot put myself in the position of my local bookseller, not because I cannot choose to abandon my academic career and sell books, but because my local bookseller did not choose to abandon an academic career.

I mention this possible interpretation in order to emphasize that my claim is intended to be understood in a less trivial sense. If we are to flourish, then we must be at peace with ourselves. If for example we find ourselves deeply ashamed of our own past, then either it is impossible for us to flourish or, at the very least, we need to come to terms with this past. In particular we cannot flourish if we continue to do what we feel guilty doing. The point about our inability to lead the lives of primitive head-hunters is that we would need to reconcile ourselves to the performance of acts that we have been brought up to view as acts of murder. We know that there are those in our society who might manage this, because our society incorporates those who are ready to commit acts of violence against others. But our society is also one in which the disposition to commit acts of violence is generally viewed as an evil which needs to be eradicated. Within the primitive tribes of head-hunters the disposition to hunt heads was not seen as a social aberration, but as something which had its proper place. So the readiness to accept the head-hunting of appropriate persons on appropriate occasions was not an indication of a culture in which any and every act of violence would have been viewed with approval. Indeed a simple appeal to the evolutionary argument which we encountered in chapter 11 should be sufficient to convince us that no such society could possibly have survived. So primitive head-hunters should certainly not be seen as psychopathic criminals.

That some people may have been able to live well in a society in which head-hunting is or was a part of the culture is no indication that we can do so if we make the attempt. If we are to live well, we need to come to terms with our problems, including our moral problems. The choice of moral principles constitutes part of our attempt to live well. The political principles we favour define a framework within which we believe we can live well in association with others. Once we are committed to such principles, they constitute our trouble-shooting strategy (see chapter 1) which we will generally be content to follow. On occasions we may find the strains of commitment so great that we fail to do so. On other occasions it may be clear to us that the strategy is failing and that we need to revise it in a way that will help confront our problems more effectively.

Our problems are then not the same as those of primitive head-hunters and we would not expect to flourish in the same circumstances as they might. This is not to suggest that cultural background determines moral or political opinions, but it colours our emotional development and predisposes us to identify particular issues as problems. We may subsequently change our minds about many things, so that for example those who are brought up as Catholics may become Marxists and *vice versa*. But the ex-Catholic Marxist can only hope not to feel troubled in performing an action that she was brought up to regard as sinful, for example practising contraception, to the extent that her present convictions seem to her to provide a basis for answering Catholic objections. The moral psychology of contraception is different for her than for the person who has never been disposed to take Catholic teaching seriously. Similarly the fact that primitive head-hunters have never felt the need to justify the practice against the objections raised by Judeo-Christian moralists means that the life that they lead is quite different from any life that *we* could ever lead.

At this point I can imagine a critic demanding to know who is meant by 'we'? 'Speak for yourself', he may say, 'but you have given me no reason to enter the magic circle of so-called rational debate in which all hinges on the demand for supposed justification and the requirements of supposed rationality, and where our morality is shaped by a need to be at peace with ourselves and a disposition to feel guilt. You may be happy to accept all these assumptions, but count me out.' My response in one way involves conceding the critic's point. We saw when we discussed scepticism that we cannot give any reason to anyone for believing or doing anything if he is totally unwilling to grant any of our assumptions about what would constitute a good reason. We equally cannot provide moral reasons that will satisfy those who are completely lacking in any capacity to feel guilt about performing actions that we hold to be wrong.

That is not however the whole story. We may also enquire about the critic's alternative. A complete sceptic would of course not have an alternative, but we have already rejected his position as unlivable. What, however, of the critic whose alternative involves a revolutionary revision of prevailing cultural norms? What can be said to the Islamic fundamentalist living in a Western pluralist society who maintains that a man who writes offensively about Mohammed should be executed or to the radical who claims that we will thrive if we dismantle the coercive power of the state since that is what leads people to behave anti-socially?

There are, I suggest, some revolutionary 'alternatives' which we have no reason to take seriously. We cannot take seriously the alternative of living the kind of life led by men and women at different times or in radically different cultures, because the life that such people have led or may still lead is not an option for us. A critic can of course offer us reasons why we ought to make important, even revolutionary, changes in particular areas, for example in our prevailing attitudes to children or elderly people or religion or education or paid employment, but he can do this only to the extent that he is willing to share *some* of our assumptions so that we have a common framework in terms of which he seeks to justify the changes that he advocates.

Some critics may however confront us with a blanket refusal to accept the assumptions of politics or philosophy. With such a critic there can be no dialogue. Of course he may claim that what he rejects is simply what *we* call politics or philosophy. But who are *we*? We are people who find ourselves affected by intellectual curiosity. We are people who were brought up to believe that certain kinds of reason are needed to justify what we and others do. We are people who as parents and teachers see no alternative to teaching others that such reasons are needed. We are people who are interested enough to pick up elementary books in political theory or philosophy. If the critic's supposed 'alternative' is one that affronts our existing susceptibilities or demands of us that we place in others a confidence we can never feel, then it is not an option for us.

At the beginning of this book, it was suggested that having recourse to a political ideology can be seen as the adoption of a trouble-shooting strategy to help us deal with or avoid difficult questions. Such strategies, it was claimed, were not confined to politics and were needed in many different areas of life to help us to handle the questions that disturb us. I also suggested that philosophy should not itself be seen as such a strategy but more as an enterprise which enables us to assess the choice of such strategies.

18

The Necessity of Philosophy?

We have seen that the fundamental assumptions of politics may be contested, and we certainly should not expect philosophy to be seen by all as a necessary activity. Those who are ready to adopt trouble-shooting strategies without feeling the need to engage their critical faculties in the selection can do so. Whether they succeed in steering clear of trouble will depend not only on the merits of the strategy, but on the confidence placed in it. To that extent a critical spirit may be less a help than a hindrance. So much is clear from contemplating Pascal's famous wager on the existence of God.[1] The wager postulates the possible existence of a God who will reward believers, but only believers, with eternal life. To those who are uncertain Pascal suggests that it is better to believe because if we believe falsely in such a God we have lost nothing that bears comparison with the prospective loss of the chance of eternal life which, if such a God exists, we will suffer if we do not believe. The problem is that, even if we accept the argument, we may not readily be able to match our fundamental beliefs to the requirements of self-interest. There may be psychological mechanisms which subtly incline us to self-interested beliefs, but we can never accept as *our* reason for a belief that it suits our self-interest.[2]

Consciousness of the disadvantages of the questioning spirit lie close to the heart of traditional conservatism's hostility to encouraging the population's disinterested pursuit of reason. For a similar reason we must not recommend the study of philosophy on the ground that it will lead those who undertake it to greater satisfaction. There can be no advance guarantee that the study of philosophy will enhance our lives or lead to the beliefs of common sense and common morality being securely anchored in our consciousness. But if there are no fruitful outcomes to the study of philosophy which can be guaranteed to the individual who is reluctant to take an interest in it, can the subject then be justified by appealing to the social benefits to which it may give rise? Does society require philosophers? Certainly the skills of philosophers are not comparable to those of lawyers, doctors, accountants or engineers. There are no tasks which can be precisely defined in the expectation that conscientious and skilled philosophers can be left to undertake them on behalf of a wider public. But this does not mean that there is no need for philosophical skills.

Just as I was ready to concede that there are many individuals to whom the study of philosophy cannot be recommended in good faith, so it would be rash to argue that every human society is one in which there is a need for philosophy. But there is a significant role for philosophy in modern societies of the kind with which we are familiar. The development of what may be called the Western way of life has been possible because of science. Here I speak deliberately of science rather than technology. What has characterized modern society is not just reliance on technology. Stone-age man after all had a technology of an unsophisticated kind, but it would be a mistake to think that we have progressed simply because we make use of a much more complex technology. Our technology is more complex because of our understanding of science. Complex technology has developed because our societies were and continue to be receptive to new ways of doing things. Because we do not take things for granted our technology is in a constant state of development. This development does not necessarily lead to the development of ever more complex technology. We may as a result of our commitment to science become so aware of some of the negative effects of the use of high technology that it is possible we shall in future opt for a simpler technology. My point however is that our social and economic lives would not have the character they do if we were not as a society respectful of the spirit of science. That spirit is not boorishly contemptuous of the past, but it is one which also insists on seeking to identify past mistakes. An Einstein, we may say, could not have emerged either in a scientific community which did not value Newton or in one which would not allow its members to criticize Newtonian mechanics.

Equally, however, the critical spirit which science demands cannot thrive if it is confined to science. The whole point of that spirit is that it cannot be contained behind a demarcation line which protects some assumptions from being questioned, or designates certain thoughts as unthinkable. We have noted how scientists like Galileo and Darwin came to challenge the assumptions of received theology. Einstein came to challenge assumptions about the nature of space and time which contradicted not merely the previous scientific consensus but also some common philosophical assumptions about the nature of time. If we wish to have innovative scientists, we have to have a culture in which men and women are able to reject the received wisdom of the past without feeling threatened.

Such a culture is one in which some people can be expected to raise philosophical questions. Amongst scientists imbued with the critical spirit, there will be those who wish to raise theoretical questions about the nature of what they do and the basis upon which they make choices. Such questions may involve considering the proper relationship between different sciences, identifying the ethical issues which relate to a decision to pursue particular kinds of research and determining when something is to be counted as a science. Similarly a culture within which a critical spirit thrives will also be one in which some non-scientists will wish to raise questions about the nature of their own activities and choices. That is why there exists, as we observed in chapter 2, the possibility of a distinctive branch of philosophy for every area of activity with its own distinctive principles and methods of argument.

I have argued only that a culture characterized by a critical spirit is one in which people who are engaged in different types of activity will wish to raise philosophical questions about their particular activities. It may be suggested that this does not establish the need for philosophy as a specialized subject with its own professional practitioners. Why for example cannot philosophy of science be safely left to interested scientists? Or philosophy of history to interested historians? In general it may be observed that my argument shows only that a culture animated by the critical spirit will be one in which many people may adopt a philosophical approach to their own particular concerns.

What such an observation overlooks is the extent to which our ability to handle philosophical questions about one subject will be reinforced by our grasp of philosophical questions that arise in other areas. For example one of the claims made in chapter 16 is that there is a structural similarity between political principles and scientific principles. In order for me to make this claim and for the reader to assess it for himself or herself, we need to think both about the nature of science and the nature of politics. So if we content ourselves with a culture in which practitioners of different arts or disciplines may readily raise philosophical questions about their own areas of expertise but in which there is no place for specialist philosophy, we are likely to lose the insights that come from the work of those who are interested in different areas of activity and who are well placed to see how ideas that arise in one area have applications in others.

The cross-fertilization that occurs between different branches of philosophy happens because, as the term *branch* implies, the subject has a structure. So although competent political philosophers must know something about practical politics, it is also advantageous for them to have some grasp of such areas as philosophy of science and moral philosophy. And just as a tree does not consist merely of a large number of branches, so the discipline of philosophy does not in its entirety consist of the philosophies of a number of other disciplines and activities. Some philosophical questions arise long before we consider the nature of specialized activities and disciplines, but in connection with any intellectually rigorous attempt to understand anything at all.

One such aspect of philosophy is formal logic, which is concerned with helping us to see when one proposition of whatever kind strictly follows from another. Another such aspect is epistemology or the theory of knowledge, which is concerned with specifying what counts as knowing a proposition. This book may have convinced readers not to assume that we can only know propositions for which we have a cast-iron proof. Perhaps there is general philosophical merit in adopting an approach in which we interest ourselves less in what propositions can be proved to be true and more in what propositions we are justified in asserting. One advantage of this approach is that we tend to be more comfortable in asserting that our moral beliefs are right or justified than we would be in claiming that they are true. If the object of our intellectual endeavours is to determine when we are justified in asserting particular propositions, then it is helpful that on political questions we commonly engage in argument with those who make fundamental assumptions which are different from our own, and who therefore will be ready to contest the assertions that we feel justified in making.

This in turn raises questions about human nature. If the test to be applied to a proposition relates to whether persons are justified in asserting it, we need to know something about the nature of these persons. We need to be clear about this since biologists may tell us that higher mammals are much more like us than previously believed, and sophisticated computers may soon be 'asserting' their own personhood. If other mammals and computers could make assertions at all, then perhaps what *they* would be justified in asserting is different from what *we* are justified in asserting. So we need to know about the perceptual and mental apparatus of those who are to count as persons. One source of such an understanding may be found in psychology. Another source may be found in the work of philosophers of language, since there may be deductions to be made about our mental apparatus from the structure of the language we use. These important questions cannot be explored here. This book seeks to show only that an interest in politics is one fairly natural route into philosophy.

Further Reading

For a survey, from the point of view of a historian of ideas, of the role that different conceptions of human nature have played in political thought, see C. J. Berry, *Human Nature*, (London: Macmillan, 1986). For a difficult but rewarding attempt to demonstrate that the rational evaluation of conceptions of justice can only take place within the assumptions of particular cultural traditions, see A. MacIntyre, *Whose*

Justice?, Which Rationality? (London: Duckworth, 1988). For a stimulating view of the relationship between philosophy and the world beyond philosophy, see R. Rorty, *Philosophy and the Mirror of Nature* (Oxford: Basil Blackwell, 1980).

Notes

Chapter 2 Political and Philosophical Thinking

1 T. Hobbes, *Leviathan*, ed. M. Oakeshott (Oxford: Basil Blackwell, 1960).
2 J. Locke, *Two Treatises of Government*, ed. P. Laslett (Cambridge University Press, 1960).
3 J. Rawls, *A Theory of Justice* (Oxford University Press, 1972).
4 R. Nozick, *Anarchy, State and Utopia* (Oxford: Basil Blackwell, 1974).
5 D. Hume, *A Treatise of Human Nature*, ed. L. A. Selby-Bigge (Oxford University Press, 1888), pp. 469–70.
6 Aristotle, *Nicomachean Ethics*, tr. W. D. Ross (Oxford University Press, 1954), p. 3.

Chapter 3 Definitions of Politics

1 Plato, *The Republic*, tr. H. D. P. Lee (Harmondsworth: Penguin Books, 1955).
2 Aristotle, *The Politics*, tr. E. Barker (Oxford University Press, 1948).
3 Ibid., p. 1.
4 Ibid., p. 5.
5 Ibid., p. 6.
6 B. Crick, *In Defence of Politics* (London: Weidenfeld & Nicolson, 1962), p. 21.
7 R. A. Dahl, *Modern Political Analysis* (Englewood Cliffs, NJ: Prentice-Hall, 1963), p. 6.
8 R. Dawkins, *The Blind Watchmaker* (London: Longman, 1986), p. 2.

9 For a discussion of differences in belief and attitude see C. L. Stevenson, *Ethics and Language* (New Haven: Yale University Press, 1944).

Chapter 4 Arguments, Reasons and Morality

1 Exchange in House of Commons on 4 June 1985. See *Official Report*, Sixth Series, vol. 80, col. 150 (Her Majesty's Stationery Office).

Chapter 5 The Status of Political Judgements

1 A cognate distinction is often drawn between *analytic* and *synthetic* truths. This relates to whether a proposition can be denied without self-contradiction.

Chapter 6 Ideology and Justification

1 New Zealand Labour Party, *1987 Policy Document*, p. 17. Mr Lange subsequently distanced himself from the policies of his Finance Minister, Mr Roger Douglas, who was the principal begetter of Rogernomics'.

Chapter 7 Economic Liberalism

1 A. Smith, *An Inquiry into the Nature and Causes of the Wealth of Nations*, Books I–III, ed. R. H. Campbell and A. F. Skinner., 2 vols (Oxford University Press, 1976).
2 L. T. Hobhouse, *Liberalism* (Oxford University Press, 1911).
3 See P. Jenkins, *Mrs Thatcher's Revolution* (London: Jonathan Cape, 1987), p. 61 and for a brief account of the relationship between Mrs Thatcher and right-wing intellectuals see H. Young, *One of Us* (London: Macmillan, 1989), pp. 407–8.
4 P. Jenkins, *Mrs Thatcher's Revolution*, pp. 60–5.
5 See D. Kavanagh, *Thatcherism and British Politics*, 2nd edn (Oxford University Press, 1990), p. 103.
6 Cited by N. Ashford, 'A new public philosophy' in *Reagan's First*

Four Years, ed. J. D. Lees and M. Turner (Manchester University Press, 1988), pp. 18–19.

7　Cited in P. Norton and A. Aughey, *Conservatives and Conservatism* (London: Temple Smith, 1981), p. 166.

8　*Get in Front Again*, Liberal Party Policy Statement (Barton, ACT: 1987), p. ii.

9　Quoted in *The Times* on Monday 23 May 1988.

10　For an account of the many different senses of the term, see S. Lukes, *Individualism* (Oxford: Basil Blackwell, 1973).

11　Interviewed in *Woman's Own* in September 1987.

12　T. Hobbes, *Leviathan*, p. 84.

13　Ibid., p. 82.

14　In para. 119 of the *Second Treatise* he suggests that 'travelling freely on the highway' constitutes tacit consent.

15　R. Dworkin, *Taking Rights Seriously* (London: Duckworth, 1977), p. xi.

16　J. Locke, *Second Treatise*, paras. 27 and 31.

17　A. Smith, *Wealth of Nations*, vol. 2, pp. 26–7.

18　A. Smith, *The Theory of Moral Sentiments*, ed. D. D. Raphael and A. L. Macfie (Oxford University Press, 1976), p. 9

19　Ibid., p. 21.

20　Nozick, *Anarchy, State and Utopia*, p. 30.

21　Ibid., pp. 32–3.

22　J. Locke, *Second Treatise*, para. 27.

23　R. Nozick, *Anarchy, State and Utopia.*, pp.176–9.

24　F. A. Hayek, *The Road to Serfdom* (London: Routledge & Kegan Paul, 1944), p. 19.

25　Ibid., p. 27.

26　Ibid., ch. 4.

27　Ibid., p. 39.

28　Ibid., p. 25.

Chapter 8　Welfare Liberalism

1　See R. Dworkin, 'Justice and rights' in *Taking Rights Seriously*, ed. Dworkin.

2　L. T. Hobhouse, *Liberalism*, p. 84.

3　Ibid., p. 77.

4　Ibid., p. 66.

5　Ibid., p. 83.

6   Ibid., p. 77.
7   Ibid., p. 75.
8   Ibid., p. 68.
9   Ibid., p. 80.
10 Ibid., p. 66.
11 Ibid., p. 80.
12 Ibid., p. 66.

Chapter 9   Arguing about Liberalism

1   The Lockean claim that man's rights are God-given may be treated as equivalent since Locke offers no arguments in support of the existence of the God who is the author of these rights.
2   See C. B. Macpherson, *The Political Theory of Possessive Individualism* (Oxford University Press, 1962).
3   R. Descartes, *Meditations on First Philosophy*, tr. J. Cottingham (Cambridge University Press, 1986).
4   For a discussion of these issues see B. Williams, *Descartes: The Project of Pure Enquiry* (Harmondsworth: Pelican Books, 1978), esp. ch. 3.
5   J. Rawls, *A Theory of Justice*, p. 145.
6   See J. Glover, *Causing Death and Saving Lives* (Harmondsworth: Penguin Books, 1977), ch. 4.
7   Rawls is an example.
8   J. Bentham, *Anarchical Fallacies*, reprinted in *Nonsense upon Stilts*, ed. J. Waldron (London: Methuen, 1987), p. 53.
9   J. S. Mill, *On Liberty*, in *Utilitarianism, On Liberty and Considerations on Representative Government* (London: Dent & Sons, 1972), p. 74.
10 See J. O. Urmson, 'The interpretation of the philosophy of J. S. Mill', *Philosophical Quarterly*, 3 (1953), pp. 33–39.

Chapter 10   The Conservative Disposition

1   These include Lord David Cecil, *Conservatism* (London: Williams & Norgate, 1912), p. 8; Q. M. Hogg, *The Case for Conservatism* (Harmondsworth: Penguin Books, 1947), p. 13; C. Rossiter, *Conservatism in America* (New York: Random House, 1962), 2nd edn, p. 6; M. Oakeshott, *Rationalism in Politics* (London: Methuen,

1962), p. 169; F. G. Wilson, *The Case for Conservatism* (University of Washington Press, 1951), p. 2.

2 M. Oakeshott, *Rationalism in Politics*, p. 168.

3 Q. M. Hogg, *The Case for Conservatism*, p. 14.

4 Ibid., p. 13.

5 Ibid., p. 11.

6 E. Burke, *Reflections on the Revolution in France* (Harmondsworth: Penguin, 1969) p. 186.

7 Q. M. Hogg, *The Case for Conservatism*, p. 16.

8 R. Scruton, *The Meaning of Conservatism* (Harmondsworth: Penguin Books, 1980), pp. 12–13.

9 Ibid., p. 25.

10 Respected television journalists were pilloried for reporting the war impartially. Later the Archbishop of Canterbury was bitterly criticized for having asked his congregation to pray for the Argentinian as well as the British dead.

11 Quoted in E. Leigh, *Right Thinking* (London: Hutchinson, 1979), p. 83.

12 Edmund Burke, *Speech on American Taxation*, quoted in E. Leigh, *Right Thinking*, p. 118.

13 Quoted in E. Leigh, *Right Thinking*, p. 119.

14 E. Burke, *Reflections on the Revolution in France*, p. 106.

15 See A. Horne, *Macmillan 1957–1986* (London: Macmillan, 1989), p. 195.

16 M. Oakeshott, *Rationalism in Politics*, pp. 188–9.

17 E. Burke, *Reflections on the Revolution in France*, p. 190.

Chapter 11   Arguing about Conservatism

1 Scruton, *The Meaning of Conservatism*, p. 26.

2 Oakeshott, *Rationalism in Politics*, pp. 177–8.

3 See Scruton, *The Meaning of Conservatism*, p. 23.

4 Ibid., p. 24.

5 Ibid., p. 187.

6 Mr Tebbit was describing his father's response to the Depression and never used the phrase in the imperative mode. See N. Tebbit, *Upwardly Mobile* (London: Weidenfeld & Nicolson, 1988), p. 187.

7 See H. J. Paton, *The Moral Law* (London: Hutchinson, 1948), p. 68. This book includes a translation of Kant's *Grundlegung*.

Chapter 12 Marxism

1 R. N. Berki, *Socialism* (London: Dent & Sons, 1975).
2 D. Miller, 'In what sense must socialism be communitarian?' in *Socialism*, ed. E. F. Paul et al. (Oxford: Basil Blackwell, 1989), p. 53.
3 This leaves women out of the picture but then Marx was no feminist.
4 In *Karl Marx, Selected Writings*, ed. McLellan, p. 202.
5 *Karl Marx, Selected Writings*, ed. McLellan, p. 569.
6 K. Marx, *The Eighteenth Brumaire of Louis Bonaparte*, in *Karl Marx, Selected Writings*, ed. McLellan, p. 300.
7 Although a different conclusion is drawn, the point is similar to one we encountered in Hobhouse.
8 K. Marx, *The German Ideology*, in *Karl Marx, Selected Writings*, ed. McLellan, p. 183.
9 K. Marx, *Capital* (2 vols, London: Dent & Sons, 1957), vol. I, p. 424.
10 K. Marx, *Economic and Philosophic Manuscripts*, in *Karl Marx: Early Texts*, ed. D. McLellan (Oxford: Basil Blackwell, 1971), p. 139.
11 Aristotle, *Nicomachean Ethics*, p. 13.
12 Aristotle, *The Politics*, p. 6.

Chapter 13 Arguing about Marxism

1 See K. R. Popper, *The Open Society and its Enemies* (London: Routledge, 1945) and *The Poverty of Historicism* (London: Routledge, 1957).
2 D. Hume, *A Treatise of Human Nature*, pp. 86–94.
3 *Karl Marx, Selected Writings*, ed. McLellan, p. 154.
4 Ibid., p. 390.

Chapter 14 A Constitutional Alternative?

1 *Socialism in England*, cited in B. Crick, *Socialism* (Milton Keynes: Open University Press, 1987), p. 68.
2 Speaking in Newcastle on 28 September 1959 and quoted in D. E. Butler and R. Rose, *The British General Election of 1959* (London: Macmillan, 1960), p. 59.

3 A. Bevan, *In Place of Fear* (London: William Heinemann, 1952), p. 170

4 Addressing the Annual Conference of the Labour Party in 1973. Quoted in D. Healey, *The Time of My Life* (London: Michael Joseph, 1989), p. 369.

5 Ibid., p. 402.

6 Quoted in D. E. Butler and R. Rose, *The British General Election of 1959* (London: Macmillan, 1960), p. 272.

7 *Platform, Resolution and Rules* (Barton, ACT: Australian Labor Party, 1986), p. iii

8 Speech to the American–European Community Association in New York on 16 April 1990.

9 See H. L. A. Hart, 'Are there any natural rights?' in *Political Philosophy*, ed. A. Quinton (Oxford University Press, 1967).

10 D. Miller, 'In what sense must socialism be communitarian?' in *Socialism*, ed. E. F. Paul et al., p. 68.

11 R. H. Tawney, *Equality* (London: George Allen & Unwin, 1931), pp. 154–5.

12 See I. Reid, *Social Class Differences in Britain*, 3rd edn (London: Fontana Press, 1989), ch. 4.

13 B. Crick, *Socialism*, p. 99.

Chapter 16 Principles and Foundations

1 J. Rawls, *A Theory of Justice*, pp. 48–51.

2 For a discussion of these issues in relation to the definition of *nation*, see A. D. Smith, *Theories of Nationalism*, 2nd edn (London: Duckworth, 1983), ch. 7.

Chapter 18 The Necessity of Philosophy?

1 B. Pascal, *Pensées*, tr. A. J. Krailsheimer (Harmondsworth: Penguin Books, 1966), pp. 149–55.

2 Pascal recognized this but argues that if we choose to perform acts of devotion, belief will naturally follow.

Index